FEARless

Buckle up ... Build RESILIENCE

TRACY TULLY

First published by Ultimate World Publishing 2020
Copyright © 2020 Tracy Tully

ISBN

Paperback - 978-1-922372-12-3
Ebook - 978-1-922372-13-0

Tracy Tully has asserted her right under the Copyright, Designs and Patents Act 1988 to be identified as the author of this work. The information in this book is based on the author's experiences and opinions. The publisher specifically disclaims responsibility for any adverse consequences, which may result from use of the information contained herein. Permission to use information has been sought by the author. Any breaches will be rectified in further editions of the book.

All rights reserved. No part of this publication may be reproduced, stored in or introduced into a retrieval system, or transmitted in any form, or by any means (electronic, mechanical, photocopying, recording or otherwise) without the prior written permission of the author. Any person who does any unauthorised act in relation to this publication may be liable to criminal prosecution and civil claims for damages. Enquiries should be made through the publisher.

Cover design: Ultimate World Publishing
Layout and typesetting: Ultimate World Publishing
Back Cover Photographer: Bel Tully   www.roguepoppystudio.com
Editor: Hayley Ward

Ultimate World Publishing
Diamond Creek,
Victoria Australia 3089
www.writeabook.com.au

She Rises from the Fire

"It's not the words of man that count, it's the words of women too; not those who deceive and delight in the failure of others, never experiencing triumph or defeat.

The praise belongs to the woman who fights the fire, rising burnt and scarred; refusing to fear her critics. The one who navigates floods, cliffs and roadblocks; facing corrupt, masked highwaymen at gunpoint.

The woman who watches, when they cut the rope of safety smiling smugly, as she plunges into the abyss.

The tribute in fact, belongs to the woman who feels the terror and trepidation of what's invisible around the corner; who suffers the pain when she gets it wrong but has the strength to pursue, because without effort, there is no failure.

She is the one who stands strong in turbulence, who struggles unaided making mistakes; who bravely travels alone.

They are the fake ones; unmotivated, dishonest, claiming their glory from those with passion; who do good deeds and have experienced the victory of great achievement.

For she fears less and dares to challenge them all."

SHE RISES FROM THE FIRE

Tracy Tully 23 April 2019

Inspired by MAN IN THE ARENA
Theodore Roosevelt, US President, 23 April 1910

Dedication

To our fearless sistas whose power of speech inspires others by courageously giving voice to the voiceless, for a more equitable future world.

I wish you continued courage and unconquerable resilience!

To my fearless referees Bel, Sam and Bob - my loyal critics and appraisers!

To my beautiful mother Joy, who is witness to a new breed of appalling government corruption, power and insatiability.

To my sisters Lindy and Caroline for their allegiance and faith in me.

To Howard Hobbs, for your unwavering support and diligent pursuit of justice under the Westminster principles governing this nation. Member Warrego Electorate held by National/LNP 1986 - 2015 (succeeded by the seat's first female member Ann Leahy).

To Mick Dowie, Detective Inspector Queensland Police Service; who ceaselessly demonstrates high ethical standards, strategic innovation, attention to detail and a firm resolve to ensure the absolute truth.

To friends and colleagues who have boldly stood by me, with their never-ending support writing this book. To Kaye Walton, Cathy Barker, and Pat Johns whose careers suffered inexcusably as a result of corrupt government officers.

I thank you

To the Queensland State Government.
It's time to review the Public Service Act and immediately adopt the practice of signed Statutory Declarations by every person who makes formal allegations against others. Stop the misuse of the Queensland Public Service Act that harmfully prevents basic human rights and natural justice, averting the truth; resulting in corrupt, deceitful, negligent behaviours and actions.

Testimonials

"Silence in the face of injustice is anything but golden. It is a free pass for those who cause suffering to continue using and abusing others for their own gain. Perpetrators of injustice usually hold positions of influence and power and speaking up against them means risking further loss, humiliation or abuse. In her book, 'FEARless' Tracy Tully writes of her personal struggle with the adversity she faced in her career and of her refusal to live a life defined by those challenges. It is an inspirational account of her strength, courage and resilience".

Nia Barnes, Psychologist
Author of 'I thought it was normal: the imprint of childhood trauma on an adult brain' (2019)

"Written in a punchy and expressive style, Tracy Tully shares her conviction that post-traumatic growth is not only possible, but within the reach of those who have suffered. Her book offers practical strategies to consider implementing through the facets of life. This book offers a fresh approach on the road beyond recovery and I congratulate Tracy on its publication".

Dr Jo Lukins, PhD.
Author of 'The Elite. Think like an athlete, succeed like a champion' (2019)

"Bullying is an insidious part of all levels of society. From early school days, during our working careers to aged care. Many are damaged by it, some are destroyed by it, most learn to cope with varying degrees of success, and a few set a shining example to others by their unfazed courage, resilience and motivation. Tracy is such a person".

**Sandra Tully, Founder of ACTIVEinspite,
Digital Alchemist, Personal Trainer
'Stay ACTIVEinspite' of what life throws at you
www.activeinspite.com.au**

"Tracy has a contagious form of enthusiasm that she generously shares. She has a way of communicating resilience techniques with joy and passion".

**Niomi Reardon, Registered Nurse, Life Coach, Educator.
Author of 'Stress Solutions. Finding your peace and inner calm'. (2019)**

#MeToo #digitaldamage #therightthingtodo
#everyonesjob #resilience #bullying

Contents

She Rises from the Fire	iii
Dedication	iv
Testimonials	vii
Welcome	xi
FEARless the Introduction	1
Chapter One: Rear View Mirror	13
Chapter Two: Road Ahead	29
Chapter Three: Calibrate your GPS	47
Chapter Four: Maintenance	61
Chapter Five: Start the Engine	73
Chapter Six: The Toolbox	85
Chapter Seven: Pot-Holes in the Road	95
Chapter Eight: Running on Empty	109
Chapter Nine: Fuel Up	121
Chapter Ten: Snap Shots	127
Chapter Eleven: Traffic Infringement	139

Chapter Twelve: Destination Known	147
About The Author	157
Acknowledgements	161
Motivation and Resilience for Women MRW	163
Speaking & Workshop Opportunities	165
Bulk Buying and Customisation	167
Bonus Offer	169
Online Programs	170
Disclaimer	172
Class Action	173
Bibliography	175

Welcome

Congratulations on your decision to purchase my book *FEARless Buckle up ... Build Resilience.*

WARNING! Don't proceed with caution!

Together we'll explore a road less travelled, a journey that motivates and assists towards building resilience and growing self-confidence, one chapter at a time.

There are many self-help groups and programmes available, but you cannot take off on a self-awareness journey unless you have the right attitude to make confident changes for yourself. YOU are the most important person today. It's vital that you get it right the first time; otherwise you'll be travelling in circles on the roundabout of life, driving on and off exits, not knowing where you're going.

One of the major issues most of us face, is finding the energy to get up in the morning and go the distance each day. What frustrates many, is how to maintain the discipline needed to build the enthusiasm to develop our physical, mental and emotional endurance. It can be difficult to acknowledge what's draining our motivation, energy, time and money. Many of us think that we can't drop all the jobs we do daily, because we believe that by doing everything, we're in control and life remains predictable, safe and secure.

What we don't see, is that we're guarding our world from falling apart, as we desperately try to protect our sanity. By doing this, we condemn ourselves to live in a world where we are constantly overwhelmed, fatigued and unhappy with our lives.

We don't understand that we're actively dumbing ourselves down, naively tolerating and accepting the chaos that we live in and by ignoring that, we park ourselves in the safety and security of our comfort zone.

We consciously prevent ourselves from stepping out into the big world of uncertainty, because of a sense of fear of the unknown. Subsequently, we hijack our lives with anxiety, sadness, indecision and fatigue, which fills us with a sense of overwhelm and ultimately, a lack of fulfilment.

Fact: if you aren't where you want to be in life, that should be enough motivation to make changes in your attitudes and habits today.

Being **FEARless** gives you permission to accept your failures, whether big or small, because everyone experiences failure in their lives. As you travel on your journey building resilience, you will learn to be brave, **FEARless** and not give a shit! There are many pot-holes

Welcome

in the road of life; tasks, encounters and challenges that we find distressing, difficult and at times bloody painful. Life comes with many trials and tests that drain our enthusiasm, passion, creativity, happiness and energy.

Pot-holes are a normal presence on our roads and these irritations, like a life crisis, bounce you around all over the place. Life regularly throws pot holes in our way, wearing away our confidence and leaving us in an existence of overwhelm hanging onto the wheel of life by our fingertips. Our fears are caused by the perception of failure, corroding our emotions and energy, creating a pot-hole, which gradually damages our self-esteem and confidence.

Our survival on this earth can be compared to roads weaving endlessly through time. Repeatedly worn down and scarred by the persistent leaching of our energy, enthusiasm and passion; through tired partnerships, poor decisions and unhappy careers chosen to 'make ends meet' for all the wrong reasons. Our existence, like traffic, gradually dissolves and erodes the surface away, requiring regular attention and repair.

Do something for yourself now, because only **YOU** can do it and no one else is going to do it for you.

It's time to be FEARless ... Buckle Up and Build Resilience.

While writing this book, I realised just how amazing it is when your life drastically changes because you stop tolerating the bullshit and start believing in yourself!

FEARless guides you to navigate the pot-holes in the road of life. As you travel through the chapters, you'll learn to road test your resilience, building self-confidence and well-being throughout your journey. Constant changes on the roadmap will test you, forcing you to recalibrate your mind compass. The secret of accepting change is to focus all your energy on building a new roadmap for your life by unleashing your creativity, diversifying and focussing on changing direction.

Your priority pledge –

I'm committed to improving myself by leveraging fear to build resilience.

Jump in, buckle up and kick the engine over! Recalibrate your life by reaching the destination you desire for yourself - **FEARless freedom!**

FEARless the Introduction

In the early hours of 12th April 2011, I received an urgent phone call warning me to download everything from my computer hard drive. I was a high school principal in a western Queensland town. Hours later, escorted from the school grounds, I was stood down on investigation for the next three years, with unknown allegations.

Alone behind the closed door to my office, there were no witnesses to what was said or done to me. Without the authority of legal documentation or explanation; my handbag was taken, contents tipped out and a box of tampons emptied with a rude comment. In full view of witness Kaye Walton my administration manager, I was 'body barged' in the hallway, by a politically groomed self-referred religious minister; to all those religious zealots that used their faith as an abusive tool against me, your time will come.

I disappeared from the place that I knew, entering a silent world of evil corruption, malicious deceit and criminal behaviours fit for a third world country. This was the 21st century and this was the Queensland Department of Education in Australia.

Trolling, cyberhate, systematic abuse and harassment all expertly delivered against me by narcissistic public servants. Well-honed tactics with the intent to frighten and threaten me into resigning, behind the pretence of a 'get them' Queensland Public Service Act PSA. The department of education uses the PSA to stand down principals under investigation. Premier of the day, Anna Bligh presided over the Qld Public Service Act changes under her administration. This allowed corruption to flourish across all government departments, in particular education and health. Government officers played the game of 'pile-on', a campaign of well organised and systematic defamation and libel against an employee. It's known by many names, and Melbourne journalist, Ginger Gorman and well-known author, Tara Moss, refer to this style of bullying as the *'dis-inhibition effect'*, where social norms don't apply - www.gingergorman.com

Two Ethical Standards Unit ESU officers ran unscrupulous interviews 'tag teaming', trying to force me to say things against my staff. I refused; they became angry; yelling and slamming the desk. It's all on tape; a collaborative effort to shame, bully and break me. Their demeanour was intent on intimidation; nasty, sarcastic, rude, loud and threatening. All evidence on tapes and transcripts held by me, clearly demonstrates their unethical behaviours. To top it all off, they boasted to me they were ex-police officers and acted as if they were in the corruption watchdog's secret Star Chamber.

FEARless the Introduction

Three interviews were conducted in 2012 during which I made a taped statement, evidence I received a fraudulent *'Directive'* signed by the Director-General, procured by these ESU officers, in a deliberate attempt to bully me. Documented evidence clearly demonstrates a criminal offence occurred when my support representative, and senior officers, had a 'tea party' discussion prior to the day of my first interview. The DG's Directive was served to me ten minutes prior to my interview. The ESU guys acted like they were police officers serving a summons; problem was, there was nothing legal to serve and standing my ground, I reprimanded them clearly on tape for their disgraceful actions, calling out their corrupt behaviours. They threw a giant toddler tantrum, raising their voices and slamming their hands on the table, storming out of the interview room. Welcome to the Queensland education department's investigative process. I issued a return letter stating that the DG's Directive was not binding, which was upheld. This cat and mouse game set the tone for a decade of unadulterated corruption. I cannot help but think how many other principals before and after me, acquiesced in unawareness when they received a similar illegal document signed by the Director General who abused their power, committing libel against me.

A union rep advised me that the DG was a lovely person. They weren't a principal under the employ of the education department and in alarm, I responded that their behaviour with me had been unhinged, unprofessional and unethical. I was advised by my senior leaders at several meetings that the DG was involved with the local town leader of the day, in removing me from my post. Furthermore, I was advised that if my husband continued to complain about the false allegations against me, I'd be removed from my school because 'the DG is sick of listening to them constantly ringing every day, complaining', evidence submitted to the Crime and Corruption

Commission CCC. The law states that my husband was well within his rights to complain, but under Labor government, the Queensland department education chose not to follow the laws; they make up their own as they go.

So, where did this story start? I was a principal managing two rural schools, primary and high at the time of the 2010 floods. As my husband and I had lost our possessions in the devastating 1990 floods, I sensed what was going to happen as I boated into town to work, the water breaking its banks upriver. It wasn't long before all hands were on deck evacuating staff members from their low-lying homes to higher ground, mustering kids and regularly informing my department of the situation.

Driving back and forth through flooded streets, between schools and staff member's homes, I continually checked on the primary school situated in the centre of town directly on a creek. It didn't take long for the situation to become critical as the water crossed into the school grounds and under buildings. I'd lived there for 24 years so was familiar with the patterns of local flooding. Twice that day, I'd requested closure of the school and been resolutely refused. Following each call, I assessed the situation with increased alarm and urgency. In those times, principals were obligated to seek authorisation to close their schools and I had no authority to send students and staff home or advertise to parents that the school grounds were under flood. I became extremely distressed when a staff member informed me, they'd driven students home sitting on the bonnet of their Toyota, through flooded streets. My decision was made. I rang the department for the third time at which stage the flood waters were at knee height and the power on. Again, I requested immediate approval to close the primary school. My request was denied, we were in a declared emergency situation and I begged my supervisor repeatedly to close the school; the response was aggressive and I was refused. I enquired as to why I couldn't close the school and was advised that the DG flatly rejected closing the schools because someone didn't want them closed and didn't want the town evacuated. If the schools had both been granted closure, many staff members would not have lost all their personal belongings, suffering years of distress, financial impact, stressed personal relationships and high anxiety. The education department negligently failed its employees in their care, during an emergency situation. This defied the Workplace Health and Safety Act and every other Act imaginable.

The 2010 floods were classified as an emergency and without approval, I was unable to authorise the school buses to shut down, the company having to make that decision themselves. Parents were unwittingly allowing their students to travel to school from four different directions each over 100kms away, through flood waters into a town that was flooding. When the buses continued to travel to school through water over the roads and with the waters rising behind them, a few council workers took the situation in hand, directing the drivers to reboard the students to urgently return them to their homes.

My responsibility was to the safety of the students and staff in my care, so on my last call to the department, I informed my supervisor that I refused the DG's directive and was closing the primary school. I reminded them of my roles and responsibilities in an emergency situation, but this conversation was not met with compassion or duty of care. I was disgusted. I evacuated the students and staff and directed the power to be turned off. I rang the local police station, informing Detective Inspector Mick Dowie Queensland Police Service of my actions and that I'd ignored the DG's directive. I told him that I'd just lost my career and he agreed with me. We were both alarmed at the gross negligence and careless regard to life.

After the floodwaters subsided and we cleaned up, I wrote a report and submitted it to an external authority; I became a whistle-blower for the second time in my career. My report triggered a wave of malicious, corrupt and deceitful behaviours and actions against me that lasted a decade. I had done the unthinkable; I had forsaken blind loyalty expected of me to my department's leader and superiors, for what I knew was clearly the right decision. I've never regretted that decision.

It's no surprise that bullying behaviours are rampant in our state schools; it's endorsed and alive from the very top levels, right down to the bottom levels of our education system. My actions did result in one great outcome; a hasty shift in the department's attitude in regards to policies in emergency situations in schools and I was relieved by the changes authorising school principals to make the decision to close their schools in emergency situations. Thankfully, the department reviewed their archaic practices and eventually, school principals were granted total authority across their schools, as they should. Local and state politicians have unquestionably no right to play God by putting children and employees' lives at such enormous risk.

During the once in a century 2020 world COVID 19 lockdown, I witnessed once again the abhorrent negligence of Queensland department of education executive leaders in regards to employees stood down on investigation. Not only had these people been totally abandoned when stood down; without any consideration to their well-being, but were treated with further neglect by the absence of contact during the entire COVID 19 lockdown. Across the globe, we witnessed the extremely high levels of anxiety, overwhelm and depression of millions of people under lockdown; it's well documented.

To be stood down on investigation by the Queensland education department PLUS locked down under COVID 19, the state of a severely affected mindset and wellbeing was unquestionably intensified with the highest level of gross negligence by a government department in the western world against an employee.

A Human Rights issue - failure to protect people in an Emergency Situation; one that will go undetected unless I give voice to the contempt department of education officers have against employee's well-being and care. At the outset of the virus lockdown, even prisoners were considered, but NOT school principals employed by the Queensland department of education on stand down; this will go down in history for this century.

Scroll back six months. I attended a high school principals' meeting, informed in dramatic hushed tones that the Deputy Director-General was implicated in the fate of principals suddenly disappearing from eastern schools, without a trace or reason. We were acutely aware that the new Queensland Public Service Act was in force; we had been advised that as public servants we no longer had protection and government employees were dropping like flies. At the time, I lived in an Australian state that was governed by a dangerous, chaotic and corrupt political Labor party, whose actions and behaviours extended to our department senior leaders – with a bent communistic compass.

I was a female regional principal, leading and managing a highly volatile and violent rural high school. I had stepped on someone's toes in a time of acute political fear and intense state government unrest; the Director General was expelled from the department, disgraced, charged and convicted of criminal offences. In a severe downhill slide, Labor party powerholders' exclusive reign on the state was imploding, further descending with each new alarming story of corruption that emerged. Flagrant unethical behaviours, corrupt actions and deceitful dealings using taxpayer's hard-earned dollars became the news of the day, as they struggled to hold their losing battle of political supremacy. At the time this book goes to print, we are once again in the same situation of political chaos, decline and economic destruction, by the same party and watching the same level of corruption coming into an election.

I lived in the Warrego Electorate, the third largest in Queensland covering 337,812 square kilometres and larger in area than Victoria and Tasmania combined, firmly established and long held by the LNP. To say my situation was political was a gross understatement. Living in the Warrego electorate proved to not only be the undoing of my career but my eventual saviour when the state changed political parties at election in 2012. But that was not to last long and once again the state spiralled into decline as party politics changed sequence in 2015.

There were many unethical government leaders who were chief influencers affecting my circumstances for the next decade and they were all powerful under the Labor Party, using their power to faithfully protect their highest members at all costs. Demonstrating greedy, narcissistic behaviours with one sole aim in mind, the pursuit of promotion for power, they sought to 'take me down'. My legal advisor explained that no resident leader in the history of Queensland had ever been involved in a principal's business, advising that it was out of order and peculiar. The reason soon became apparent to us all, the upcoming election and expectation by the Labor Party to win the vast Warrego electorate seat. My story is about political corruption at the highest levels and all about votes. A story suitable for a motion picture.

I was left without contact, unsupervised and with no documentation or information on what I had supposedly done or what was going to happen to me. I eventually learned that this was a calculated and well-practised method that provided the Ethical Standards Unit ESU with the advantage of time, to aggressively pursue and coerce others to 'make allegations against me', to strengthen their arguments, giving their purpose more power and dramatic effect.

It was bizarre. I was treated like a criminal but with no criminal charge against me. Unable to speak to anyone and locked away from the world under the Queensland Public Service Act, granting immense power to the Education Department's exclusive and unethical 'house arrest'. I was not allowed to travel anywhere over three days without giving notice. It took me two days to return travel from my closest regional city. I was forbidden from leaving the country and was trapped in my house 1,200kms from Brisbane. All without any reasons. I was living in the 21st century in a democratic country run by a department of political powerbrokers - it was socialism.

I had no communication with family, friends or colleagues and no knowledge of what was happening to me. I was 'watched and regularly reported on' by coerced employees who were questioned about the ownership of cars parked in my driveway. Isolated in our home five kilometres from town, my health, well-being and mental state began a rapid downward spiral, much like that of our state's chaotic political party of the day.

Dark depression and acutely high anxiety increased uncontrollably and for the following three years, there was barely any communication from my department. When I did finally receive communication, it was militant, aggressive and without controls; 'free for all and anything goes' department practices were undetected by the Crime and Corruption Commission CCC, and still is the case to this day.

Traumatised and living in a constant state of high alert, I failed to find any legal documentation that justified my treatment. Of course, there wasn't any!

My husband, an itinerant worker who travelled in isolated areas and interstate for lengthy periods of time, was forced to take extensive time off work to stay with me. Our children were in boarding school and I was unable to visit or help them understand what was happening to their mother; an archaic Queensland government department's strategy to break people and these practices are still very much alive today. Like its leadership and management - living in the Industrial Age.

I plunged into a bottomless tunnel of disturbing paranoia and intense fear for my safety. My mind and body declined rapidly and mental health deteriorated at an alarming rate. The anguish and torment were alarming for my family, especially my aged mother. I was in a high state of constant alert and became sick, suffering rapid weight and hair loss, permanent nerve damage to the right-hand side of my face; ear, mouth and eye. I have permanent physical and physiological effects resulting in significant dental, facial and health problems and restorative surgery. The department has no policy in place to deal with this and is devoid of anyone with the expertise or authority to either lead or manage it. A bizarre, modern day system of torture, worthy of prime-time television.

FEARless the Introduction

Through the fog of opioid medication, I knew I had to regain control of my life and preserve the lives of our tragically affected children. The Queensland education department, charged with the responsibility for the safety of all children, had absolutely no care for their wellbeing and safety, ignorant to the horrific brutality wielded on others, within its corrupt leadership. Our children's lives were ruined by the power this department vested in others, who were intent on using malicious conduct for their own political gains.

Several of my employees and those considered my 'friends', were dismissed from their roles in my school, their lives and that of their families upended without any warning; all suffered financial strain as a result. Together with my family, they were the 'collateral damage' targeted by a tsunami of hate and isolation. Their alarming stories started filtering to me. I was disturbed at the calculated cruelty handed out by senior officers, public servants with egos, greed and the need for immense power at any cost. This behaviour continues to this day and as I write, principals are fighting back against the continued corruption by department personnel. I know this because they find me on the internet asking for help, support and guidance in a bid to understand these atrocious behaviours and actions by their government department leaders.

It was 'thrive or dive', so I chose to fight back.

I left our forever home to undergo lengthy medical procedures to repair my body's physical and physiological damage over the next two years. I was forced to endure the ranting threats of a corrupt senior education official who was appointed Acting Director-General for five days over Christmas and who relentlessly tried to prevent me from accessing my basic human rights – medical care. I was required to have surgery and he did everything in his power to prevent it, questioning my doctor's credentials and demanding a letter from my doctor stating all his qualifications, despite having received the necessary documentation. Each time I was forced to return to the doctor to satisfy this mad man's needs, it cost me money. The medical profession is well versed in dealing with the education department. When he failed to prevent a medical procedure going ahead, he instructed that I provide all the intricate details of my medical condition, the medication I was on and why I was having surgery in Toowoomba and not Brisbane! He demanded I front up to the investigators immediately following my surgery which was a little bit difficult when you're confined to a hospital bed. He was a complete and utter bloody idiot, in charge of the entire department and responsible for thousands of students and employees. The problem is, there are many of them.

This journey of unfettered and dangerous political power and corruption forced me to move forward in life and my future. This book emerged from the ashes of my career, helping me through the challenge of political corruption. As a two times whistle-blower, I chose resistance.

CHAPTER ONE

Rear View Mirror

"Fear is the main source of superstition, and one of the main sources of cruelty. To conquer fear is the beginning of wisdom".

Bertrand Russell

How often have you felt fear? Does fear stop you from pursuing the things you wish you could do in your life? Fear can keep us from harm, or it can become an inner voice that causes us to make poor decisions or stop us from participating in activities we would like to pursue.

What is fear?

"An unpleasant emotion caused by the threat of danger, pain or harm". "Be afraid of (someone or something) as likely to be dangerous, painful or harmful". English Oxford Living Dictionary

What an understatement! I wouldn't call fear 'an unpleasant emotion'. Fear controls our minds and paralyses our decision making. It gives us a false sense of being, distorting our reality. Living with prolonged fear causes permanent physiological damage to the body. I live in a constant state of high alert, it's permanent and governs every waking minute of every day, this relentless anxiety has led to very high blood pressure.

What causes fear?

"Fear is a feeling induced by perceived danger or threat that occurs in certain types of organisms, which causes a change in metabolic and organ functions and ultimately a change in behaviour, such as fleeing, hiding or freezing from traumatic events". https://en.wikipedia.org

"Fear in human beings may occur in response to a certain stimulus occurring in the present, or anticipation or expectation of a future threat, perceived as a risk to body or life. The fear response arises from the perception of danger leading to confrontation with or escape from / avoiding the threat, which in extreme cases of fear can be a freeze responses or paralysis". En.Wikipedia.org/wiki/Fear

ABS figures show that heart disease, Dementia, Alzheimer Disease, vascular, respiratory diseases and diabetes are among the leading causes of death in Australia. 3303.0.55.003 -*Changing Patterns of*

Mortality in Australia, 1968-2017 Australian Bureau of Statistics 30/11/2018

The term 'mental health' is often used to describe conditions such as depression, anxiety and PTSD. The World Health Organisation (WHO) views mental health as a 'state of well-being'. It's about what's going well, rather than what's the problem, it's about wellness rather than illness.

The benefits of positive mental health increases learning, creativity, productivity, positive social behaviour and relationships, improved physical health and morality. Mental health is about being cognitively, emotionally and socially healthy.

"Around 1 in 6 women in Australia will experience depression and 1 in 3 women will experience anxiety during their lifetime". www.beyondblue 2019. These figures increase annually.

Women are well known for being nurturers and it's no surprise they put others first, so when it comes to women's health, it's imperative that women learn to prioritise their own needs, speak up and seek help when they need support.

Looking back

Do you ever find yourself thoughtfully driving along, peering through the Vaseline-coated lens of time, gazing wearily into the rear-view mirror at the history of your life? When you return your focus to the windscreen in front of you, do you find that you quickly comprehend with alarming clarity, that 'this is it, this is my life'? You're experiencing a moment in time 'prompt' and will probably ask yourself, 'is this all there is to my life'? Many people experience this moment in time 'prompt'; those who've studied hard, worked long hours in a career without thanks, nurtured and raised a family and seem to never have enough money to take a long holiday. These people are constantly tired and feel fear that they cannot see a way forward or out of 'the rut', that has become their life.

Do you see a future stretched out in front of you like a dark, dismal, never-ending highway on a rainy night? When you peer through the flip-flopping of the rubber wiper blades, swishing at the pounding droplets of rain drizzling down on the cold, foggy glass, do you feel fear? When you feel that first frightening glimpse, the tightening grip in your chest and the realisation that 'this is it'; do you find yourself questioning your life with the words 'Is this as good as it gets'? Then you're feeling fear, experiencing a moment in time 'prompt'. I call it a 'life crisis' as opposed to a life crisis, which is more about a traumatic experience.

Some people often refer to their anxiety as experiencing a life crisis, a time when small hills turn into great mountains. Some even describe their hardships as comparable to a horror movie, played out in front of them on a theatre-sized movie screen, powerless to grab the remote and press the stop button. A catastrophe of this enormity slams you face-first into a brick wall with such gravitational force that your life's journey is permanently etched onto your face! That hurts; it hurts your pride, values, sensitivity, principles and more importantly, your future plans.

If you're a glass-half-empty person, then you'll be feeling sheer fear, but if you're a glass-half-full kind of person, always looking for the positive in every negative situation, a crisis or life breakthrough can provide you with the perfect opportunity to recognise what you want in life, what is meaningful to you and what is realistic for you.

I choose to view a crisis as a life breakthrough, a rough road which needs to be branded with its own unique term and recognised as a significant watershed in one's life. Rake through all the raw tenderness, pain and fatigue and look closely at what messages that crisis can teach you. It's a little like reading your horror scope!

When we're 'up to our neck deep in it', inevitably we find ourselves calling on the big guy upstairs. Whether a believer or not, one must call on someone for all the answers! You know it, you've been there, you wouldn't be reading this book if you hadn't been in this situation at one time or another, or else you're really nosy and one of my perps!

Unlike theistic religions, in Buddhism there is a non-belief in a creator God. There is no reliance on an external agent for one's salvation; it's considered that only **we** can save ourselves. It's all about taking responsibility for ourselves. Only **we** hold the solution to our problem. Ring any bells? Sound familiar? Did you hear a big person say that way back in primary school when you were a kid?

For many people, this is way too complicated; it's so much easier to hand over responsibility to someone or something else external to ourselves. It's called **BLAME** and it happens around us every day. Too often throughout my career, I saw nasty public rage using sniper tactics aimed through the crosshairs of anger and pointed directly at those who were deemed helpless, shooting them down. Outside work I see bullying in hospitality; mostly young people, teenagers at school, ill-equipped and innocent of the life skills required to handle hardened, habitual whingers and whiners.

Those stubborn, whinging, whining complainers who grumble and nit-pick about everything are dedicated to being heard; loudly critical and always hiding behind the "click, like, tag" social media culture to gain precious attention to themselves. This group of irritating natives with chips on their boring shoulders are constantly dissatisfied. You'll find them easily because they carefully clutch their shawl of misery closely around their shoulders. They stick out in the crowd wearing a sour, devious look on their grouchy faces and for those of us in the know, you can pick them approaching a mile off! Your bullshit monitor bellows loudly! My department was full of them.

These grouchy, sullen natives are a truly rare breed of an exotic tribal species, with no hope of extinction anytime soon! Resentful, jealous, bitter and envious, all badges they wear with pride and immense self-satisfaction. They cannot see a problem and then look for a solution to make it go away. No, these tribal natives pass the problem parcel on like a hot potato, offloading onto everyone else. Do you know someone like this? Of course, you do, they're toxic!

The key from a Buddhist point of view, is that as human beings, we have self-awareness that enables us to enter our own minds and take responsibility for what is going on in there. Our inner mental self influences how we act which in turn determines the course of our lives. Many people react to external situations in an unconscious and customary manner with emotions such as indignation, fear, anger and confusion.

If we learn to create a gap between the stimulus and our immediate reaction, then we successfully learn that we have choices about how we can respond more productively. We start to learn to react with clarity. Buddhist monks are mentored and trained in it over many years. Gradually we can change how we respond to situations.

In the long term, our personality expands creatively, so what we dwell on we become. If we habitually react to situations angrily and 'stew on it', that's what we become – angry and hypercritical. Buddhist monks we are not.

Hindsight beats foresight every time. If only we all had 'the sight', a crystal ball to periodically gaze into our lives and tweak the necessary adjustments to keep our existence orderly, neat and tidy. We would see clearly where our life breakthrough fits snuggly into our life journey – with hindsight.

We pray for luck following a life-altering crisis, often viewing it as our own personal failure. Not every life breakthrough pushes us towards a rainbow on the horizon, as many self-helpers would like you to think. Just how many people do you know personally who are living the dream?

Failure is life's feedback. Without it, you couldn't improve as a person, and in turn, your life wouldn't be richer for it. There is no age limit to receiving life's feedback. We are forever learning if we keep listening to the teaching. I have regularly observed that high achievers are confident people and confident people are successful people. Success is the accolade others give you, but it doesn't last forever. As one very dear colleague once told me as she congratulated me for my achievements, "There is only one way to go from the top Tracy – and that is straight to the bottom!" She was correct.

I've reached my breakthrough in life and I'm confident enough that I don't need to pamper any minority, or for that matter, majority groups. I only need to pamper myself! I don't have to be frightened of my unique oneness anymore. It's like see-through tampon wrappers; you don't have to disguise what's in the package because it might offend someone.

Attitude is a big part of your life breakthrough, this life-changing period you've been experiencing. Without a good dose of attitude, life will get in your way, trip you up and slap you hard across the back of your head, rudely pushing you forward into the next chapter of your life, with or without your consent. The 'good old days' are just that – old and past. It's the present we're living in. So why do we so often ignore it, wishing it will go away?

Sometimes, it only takes a single event of mammoth proportion to shove you through the gates of hell. It's during these difficult times that you will experience the most terrifying emotions of absolute fear, crippling anxiety and utter isolation. Fear will paralyse you, thwarting your ability to think rationally and preventing you from helping yourself or even seeking help. Fear is your inner voice that keeps you trapped in a dark place you cannot seem to escape. Fear makes us feel helpless.

In each chapter, you will read an example of one of my life breakthrough events and you'll begin to understand why it's so very important to recognise that there's a lot at stake if you don't take matters into your own hands. So, buckle up and learn how to build your resilience.

A story of hell

At the age of ten, a beautiful, gentle and happy ten-year-old boy contracted Meningitis. He was hospitalised and extremely unwell for a very long time. It was a harrowing time for his parents, who helplessly watched doctors administering bucket loads of fluids intravenously in every place possible, even between his toes. His head and neck continued to ache many months after being discharged from hospital and he suffered numerous ongoing effects of the illness that inevitably left his body weak, fatigued and in pain. There was a lengthy rehabilitation recovery period and his parents were warned there would be side effects following this. He experienced excessive fatigue, painful headaches and very high body temperatures. He couldn't go outside in the sun, his tendons stretched and his legs ached incessantly. There was a possibility he could lose his hearing, he needed to drink copious amounts of water daily and rest regularly. The list went on.

Eventually, he returned to school. His parents discussed with the principal and classroom teacher the boy's need to be excused to access the bathroom during class time as this was part of his recovery from Meningitis. They provided information and pamphlets from the hospital. The teacher seated the students in groups, the boy's group was at the front of the classroom. The teacher in their wisdom, chose to seat him with his back to the board; requiring him to constantly twist and turn around, causing him immense neck pain - his neck and body sore and weak. The teacher used a reward system; if a student needed to leave the room to go to the toilet, the group was penalised. The boy's group was regularly penalised. The other kids became angry at his regular trips to the bathroom; the boy became ostracised, embarrassed and anxious. He struggled going to school each day. The bullying continued, aided by the classroom teacher who failed to acknowledge that her reward system was discriminating against his medical issues and therefore, not only was she condoning the bullying against the sick child, she was instigating it.

One afternoon, the boy was waiting for the school bus to pick him up outside the school gate. The bus stop was not supervised that day as the principal rostered on, failed to attend. The young boy, along with many other school students, waited for one of the four buses that drove him daily to and from school in the four directions of the compass. He travelled on the western bus every afternoon. This beautiful young boy was our son.

Three hours earlier that day, a senior student at my school started a fight; his last vicious school fight in a long series of physical abuse against other students. He demonstrated the effects of an illegal substance. His face, eyes, body and actions all indicated he was under the influence of an illicit substance. I was in the process of advising him that I was cancelling his enrolment at school when he ripped off his shirt, yelling at me with spit flying out of his mouth, 'I'll f@#n bash you, you f@#n bitch. Come on c@#t, do you want a fight? I'll f@#g bash you, you f@#g c@#t, I'll f@#g bash your kids too'.

I instructed him to leave the school and escorted him out. He stormed out of the building, swearing and threatening anyone who poked their heads out as he went. I watched him disappear from the school grounds. I rang his mother, she said she was coming to see me. She arrived angry, highly agitated and clearly demonstrating the effects of drug use. Horrifyingly, she was carrying a foster baby in her arms. She swore and yelled at me, threatening to bash me, bash my kids, shoot my dogs and burn my house down. Further threatening her husband would bash me, my husband, kill the dogs and burn the house down. I escorted her out of the admin building screaming and swearing abuse. When I returned to my office, her husband rang. He also yelled the same violent threats against my children, dogs, house and husband.

Shortly after, a teacher rang notifying me that the student was heading up the road towards the school, with a large angry mob of drunk men. I rang the police who advised me there was a funeral in town and the men had been drinking since morning, I engaged the school in immediate lockdown. I ran through the school advising it wasn't a practice and then crossed onto the oval near the front fence to meet the police. The drunken mob surged up the street towards the school, jumping the fence, yelling as they walked towards me. The police hadn't arrived, so I went to a remote area of the school oval as far away from the students and classrooms as possible. I rang the police constantly for backup. I knew not to face the mob, keeping my back to them. I could hear them close behind me. I could feel the student breathing on my neck, yelling in my ear and swearing at me, demanding that I fight him.

The school bell sounded the end of the day. The staff had expertly ushered the students off the grounds and out of sight to the buses and parents who were waiting. The student's sister appeared next to me, crying and yelling at her brother to stop, pleading and screaming at him not to hit me because he was old enough to go to jail. Eventually, to my immense relief, the police came and dealt with the situation. I went back to my office to contact my supervisor and lodge my reports.

My phone rang, it was our son; he was crying uncontrollably. He had been physically attacked at the school bus stop by a group of kids. I quickly rang my boss, told him what happened and that I was going home and couldn't finish my report. While driving home, my boss rang telling me to take our son straight to the police station and hospital, he'd arranged to expect us. I was exhausted, sobbing and sickened at what they had done to our son. I arrived home to find him terrified, bruised and bleeding. He was ten years old. His head, face and lips were cut, his eyes black and swollen. He had bruises all over his body - up and down his front, over his back and buttocks. The principal on duty had failed to appear and not one single adult came to his rescue at the bus stop for fear of getting involved with the parents that had driven the kids to the school gate to oversee bashing the principal's kid.

The drug-crazed mother had collected her 17-year-old son, his mates and their mothers, and together they drove to our son's school. The mothers 'supervised' while their kids took turns bashing our son, holding him up against the school fence. Payback because I excluded a violent student from school.

At the police station, our traumatised son gave his statement before we headed to the hospital. I told the officer about the threats I'd received earlier that day and reported the mother was under the influence of drugs and had a foster baby in her care. The police officers drove to their home, found the drug-related items, removed the baby from her care and charged her and her husband. They left town immediately. I was informed that I did not have to attend court as they'd admitted to all the offences and would be convicted. The local police officer in charge was exemplary, supportive and caring, ensuring that the situation was dealt with swiftly and professionally.

That evening, our son begged me not to send him back to school. He pleaded with me to go to boarding school. He left home at the end of Grade 5. A year later, several of my staff and parents complained to the department that my kids went to boarding school and not to the local public school and how disgraceful that was. The department officers agreed with them - how dare I enrol my kids in a private school, what sort of public-school principal was I? Those government officers had no knowledge or understanding of the circumstances or meaning of choice, safety and care that we needed to provide our kids because of our jobs in schools in violent towns. Nor did they have any idea whatsoever what it was like to be a principal in that town. Not one of them had ever done service in a school like this one. For those parents who deemed it appropriate to whinge to the department that I sent my kids to boarding school, half of them sent their kids to boarding school and some of the staff members did too! For those staff, a complaint would get them a promotion out of town! They all made committed libel by making false allegations that they'd left because of me; however, they had all informed me their reasons, prior to leaving because of the lack of football and the rising town drug and alcohol fuelled violence.

Years later when our kids had grown up and left home, my husband and I were enjoying a coffee on our back veranda when a car drove slowly into our back yard. Inside the car was a family with young children. A man got out and walked up to us. I asked my husband if I was seeing correctly and was this who I thought it was? He nodded. The young man stopped not far from us. My husband greeted him, asking what he wanted. Turning to me, the young man apologised for everything he'd done to me, our family and for the way he'd behaved at school. He said he was off the drugs, married with children and had nothing to do with his mother or any of his family. He then advised us that he was renting a house two doors down the road. I was horrified.

The outcome of this story is a good one though. That young man remained true to his word, appearing to be a good partner to his wife and father to his children. He never harassed me. He brought his family over to meet me a month later, so proud of being a father. Most kids in crisis are reacting to their environment - take them away from that environment and they will blossom.

It was during this traumatic time in our lives that I found great care and kindness. My supervisor at the time, Regional Director Mike

Ludwig, was an exemplary leader, highly professional, efficient and a terrific principal mentor. Mike Ludwig was the last of the great education leaders in our region. Highly professional, organised, caring and compassionate, he held his staff in the highest regard and likewise they reciprocated their respect for him. His actions and behaviours were always of a high standard. He eventually chose to return to principalship. While he was running our region, it was excelling at every level but after he left, we watched knowingly, as up to 20 acting senior leaders flowed in and out of our area of the region. Not one of them would stay because as they explained to me - of the chaos and bullying that was rife in the regional offices.

Everything was done with the utmost care for our traumatised 10-year-old son, who was physically abused and terrified by a student who was not deemed an adult by age but who wielded the strength and viciousness of physical assault of an adult against a child. Aided and abetted by their mothers, this was a common occurrence in our town. Too often senior staff and I would view video footage online of students fighting after school within a ring of cars near the river, parents shouting and cheering them on. It was no wonder that these kids brought to school with them daily, an attitude of fighting, applauded by their parents at home.

I never again witnessed or worked with a highly professional and supportive supervisor. With the departure of one great leader came the arrival of one corrupt, sexist and abusive leader. Our department changed overnight and with it, the chaos and decline became obvious in clearly diminished academic results across our region.

I asked for a transfer out of town, due to the situation with our son, but was deliberately denied. Sexist and openly discriminatory, I was told that, "only men should be principals in this school', yet despite that comment, I was denied a transfer. I remember his introduction at a principals' conference, greeting us all for the first time, his opening line was, 'I know it seems like we're communist, but we're not, it just looks like that'. You had to be kidding me, the DG's henchman had arrived, and was well groomed.

Bullying in Australia happens everywhere; in our schools, our workplaces and our homes. Parents and school staff struggle daily to cope with incidents of bullying. Anyone can be a victim of bullying, regardless of their age. It is a pandemic in Australian schools.

With increased internet use, a higher percentage of girls report cyber-bullying each year. It takes significant human resource personnel, who are notoriously time-poor, both during and after work hours, to manage behaviour incidents including lengthy interviews, school and department report writing, phoning parents - usually after hours, notifying the department when decisions are made to suspend or exclude, and managing all parties involved.

How do we learn to overcome trauma or bullying? How on earth do we move forward from fear in our lives and feel the freedom to laugh again? The answer is in this book. Keep reading to find out how, because if I can, you can too!

Did you know that our thoughts sabotage how we view our day, starting when we wake up in the morning? They trigger biochemical reactions in our brain, releasing chemicals that make the body mirror the way we feel. Knowing this information helps us to recognise that in order to help ourselves think positive thoughts, we need to target how we think from the moment we wake up in the morning.

End of Chapter Activity

To help you start your day on a positive note, here is my list of 5 micro habits you can do first thing every morning to clear your mind!

FIVE MICRO HABITS

1. Wake up, roll straight onto your back and stretch your body full length. Take five deep breaths inhaling through your nose, exhaling through your mouth. This clears your lungs of stale air and gets the blood pumping. It also signals your brain that you're in control, preventing you from worrying about the time and whether you're running late for work or not!
2. DRINK a glass of room temperature water left by your bedside and go to the bathroom.
3. After the toilet do five deep squats making sure your bottom is pushed out behind you.
4. At the sink wash your hands and clean your teeth. Say an affirmation by looking in the mirror and telling yourself 'It's going to be a great day today!'
5. Follow with 5 arm lifts with 1kg weights (you can use two sauce bottles if you can't afford the weights and increase the weight as you feel comfortable).

By leveraging these 5 Micro Habits alongside common morning activities; getting out of bed, going to the bathroom, cleaning your teeth etc, you'll start a focused morning routine. You'll find that you increase your ability to control your mind from negative thoughts and your legs and arms will get stronger every day! You will also find that every time you go to the toilet, if you do five squats over the course of a day, you'll increase your core strength with this one single micro habit!

CHAPTER TWO

Road Ahead

"To have greater self-awareness or understanding means to have a better grasp of reality".

Dalai Lama

Do you find that listening to the daily news makes you feel depressed and overwhelmed with all the trouble around the nation, the world and even your own 'backyard'? This messes with our self-awareness, our belief in ourselves.

At times in life when we're feeling overwhelmed and stressed, we blame anyone but ourselves for our misery and try to control others, even when it's against our best interest to do so. We live in a world that has a culture more interested in destroying relationships than preserving them.

Fear is only as deep as we allow it to be and to prevent fear from getting its tentacles into our brain, we must learn self-awareness. We can beat fear so don't let fear into the driver's seat; toss it in the boot. Before embarking on your new journey, you must be in control of your emotions, decision making, behaviours and actions. If you let fear inside the vehicle with you, you'll never take off the hand brake, you'll lack the courage to be a safe traveller on the roads and your fear will make you a risk to other drivers around you.

Do you know someone who's recovering from a broken relationship, who won't give up trying to feel good but continues to search for happiness in ways that don't involve relationships; through alcohol, food or drugs? These people are without 'self-awareness'.

> *"One of the greatest discoveries a man makes, one of his greatest surprises, is to find he can do what he was afraid he couldn't do".*
>
> **Henry Ford**

Surprise yourself and give up an addiction such as smoking.

The beliefs and assumptions that we have about ourselves and others are central to our well-being as they govern our behaviour. They can be positive or negative. Our values determine so much in our lives such as our standards, morals, ethics and the principles that guide us daily.

Developing our self-awareness involves a lifetime journey to achieve and it's the foundation of our personal growth and success. As we learn more about ourselves, we build an impenetrable foothold on which we can stand confidently. Confidence gives us the courage to build new life experiences, creating opportunities which expand our knowledge and understanding, ultimately improving our ability to respond to change with the willpower to succeed.

Our success in life relates to how well we're involved in growing relationships with others; in our workplace, homes, raising our kids or in public. Unhappiness can lead us in one of two directions; we can either try to improve our relationships or we give up on finding happiness and developing good relationships. The second group doesn't give up on trying to feel good, but they search for happiness in other ways that don't require the complexity of nurturing good relationships; such as abusing drugs, alcohol, violence or unwanted sex. This group consciously chooses to self-destruct, making them toxic to others.

Usually when people are unhappy, they talk as if they're fulfilled, but this assumption is wrong, it's only talk. They fail to find gratification, so it's much harder to help them. Whether they like it or not, they must meet happy people to find happiness. We have more success if we seek relationships with positive people. Like-minded people bring out the best in themselves and others, because they want to develop successful relationships.

Finding your 'why not'

To me, finding my 'why' creates an immediate expectation that there should be a rational explanation for everything that we do in life. Sometimes, we act in ways which we can't explain, even to ourselves. So, if we don't know how to find our 'why' then 'why not' look for something else?

I find that as I get older, people are less inclined to be cautious about asking my age. It's as if ageing gives others a licence to be intrusive. When asked, my answer is simple; 'forever juvenile'! It has the desired effect, it's a real conversation stopper! Why not?

Too often, people struggle to say the word 'no', especially women who are recognised as nurturers and tend to be people pleasers. Saying 'no' is simple. Try saying it in different tones, with different accents and in different languages. It's a highly-recognised, universal word, so why is it, that so many people struggle to utter the word 'no'? Saying 'no' puts yourself first and others in second place. It's non-conditional. 'No', is a no-fuss statement and doesn't require an explanation. Try saying it with a side-to-side nod of the head, close your eyes and raise your eyebrows at the same time. There, you've done it!

The word 'no' is one of the easiest words to learn in the English language. It doesn't need to be accompanied by any other words; it's strong enough to sit all on its own. The problem is, we struggle saying the word 'no' because we believe that saying 'no' will result in conflict or confrontation. So, "what part of 'no' don't you understand"?

Finding our 'why' is about discovering our self-awareness. *'Self-awareness is the conscious knowledge of one's own character and feelings'*. Awareness is the *'knowledge that something exists or understanding of a situation or subject at the present time, based on information'. Cambridge English Dictionary*

It's about having a clear insight into our strengths, weaknesses, personality and emotions. Developing our self-awareness gives us the ability to learn more about ourselves, which in turn, guides us to understand what we can achieve in our lives.

Do you have self-awareness? It's the ability to take a good, long, hard honest look at yourself, without falling apart and becoming fearful of what you find!

> *"The only thing we have to fear, is fear itself."*
> **Franklin D. Roosevelt**

If you're reading this book and have experienced discouragement and failure, then you're on the right track to discovering your self-awareness. Self-awareness allows you to learn from your mistakes and equally importantly, from your successes. Every single person is on a road of 'finding oneself' but not in a hippy, cosmic kind of way. They might be at different milestones on the road, but they're all on one road in life.

Self-awareness is achievable for everyone and if you drive along the road less travelled with me, then you need a good dose of self-awareness on board. You're going to discover your 'why?' and with absolutely no competition from anyone else. 'Where do you find it?' I hear you ask. Too often, it's the most terrifying challenges in life that provide us with the greatest growth, biggest inspiration and extreme experiences. You must take risks in your life and career if you are to succeed.

Live your life like a road trip, a journey that's full of stops, turns and treacherous potholes along the way. Whether you realise it or not, it will all work out in the end. Trusting the vehicle in which you're travelling is the attitude you rely on toward confident driving. Navigating the unknown is difficult for most people, especially if you don't feel confident.

"Face your fears early in life – they only grow bigger if you don't embrace challenges."
Annie Crawford, Founder & Director of CAN TOO

Finding your self-awareness

To embark on any road-trip of self-growth, you must be well prepared. You need a good attitude, confidence and self-awareness to protect you from any calamities you might encounter. You will grow those capabilities by drawing on your knowledge and driving skills. It's your ability to understand and read a situation.

I remember a time before I sat for my driver's licence, my father took me onto a large claypan. It had rained, the ground muddy and slippery. An ex-defence force officer, my Dad instructed me quietly and seriously to drive in large circles, changing gears and increasing my speed as I went.

The inevitable happened. The car started skidding and sliding in the mud and he taught me what to do; 'feel the car in your hands, don't fight it, don't grip the wheel, squeeze the brakes, don't jerk it, relax and enjoy driving in the mud'. We spent a couple of hours mud driving, narrowly missing trees and laughing, even though I was gripping the wheel so hard my fingernails cut my palms! At the end of my driving lesson he smiled at me. He was aware of my personality and sought the confirmation he needed that I was fearful and respectful of the situation I was driving in. He knew me better than I knew myself, because I was and always will be, a risk-taker. Over the years, forced into tough situations where I needed to control my car in mud, gravel, floods, sand and snow, I thanked him for those lessons, many times.

My parents left me a legacy by preparing me for my future. The day came soon enough using split-second decision making, to prevent myself from rolling my vehicle. I have passed that legacy onto our kids, to understand that while you experience fear, you do not have to let it own you, your actions or your behaviours. Rehearse the feeling of fear, familiarise yourself with the mind talk that will sabotage your actions. When your mind is confident, fear will diminish. This is how you develop self-awareness.

Feeling fear is not always a bad thing. It forces you to appreciate and understand situations and experiences, helping you to either cope with them again and again, or avoid them altogether. Sometimes, you just don't have the choice. Fear is an emotion that when mastered, helps build strong resilience. Fear is part of the 'fight or flight' response. Sometimes you only need to learn a lesson once to gain a valuable experience which provides you with greater insight into how you react in certain situations.

> *Each time you feel fear, you become more skilled at understanding a deeper level of yourself. You have insight into your immediate reactions to unknown situations. When your mind is confident, fear will diminish. It is then, that you will discover the power of self-awareness.*
> **Tracy Tully**

The more you observe, participate in and undergo difficult circumstances, the greater your level of insight into your self-awareness develops. With disciplined self-focus, you can learn to better understand how to predict unpleasant people, situations or events. You learn how to read the environment around you and how people react when they're drunk, high, angry, annoyed, irritated or sad.

Eventually you learn to become desensitised to unguarded reactions. You don't need to climb a mountain, sit in a cave or fast for two weeks to 'find yourself'. You can learn the strategies that will help you analyse your personality, actions and behaviours right here in my book.

Immediately after graduating from school, my husband advised both our kids that they needed to spend time working in a pub. This experience is important for a young person about to enter the volatile adult world of pubbing and clubbing. On their first day, the publican led them to the front door and asked them to take a good look at the customers sitting at the bar. He proceeded to enlighten them about the importance of carefully watching people, what they were doing and how they behaved and to observe the various personality traits and habits of people. Bel and Sam would come home after work regaling us with hilarious stories of customers and their personalities. The lesson wasn't lost on them and they are better people for their time spent behind the bar serving, rather than at the bar drinking!

When you're able to relax and self-analyse your personality and reflect on your actions, reactions and behaviours, you will start to understand yourself, ultimately helping you to better prepare for a variety of situations in your life. Only then will you manage to find your 'why' and understand that 'self-awareness' is central to improving our lives. It's important to not only be aware of yourself, it's also important to learn to observe others. Until you have done this, you won't be able to appreciate or understand how people react to your personality or how they might perceive you. This skill is not an easy one and I challenge you to be honest and brutal with yourself!

We often think that self-criticism is the key to self-improvement, pushing ourselves to perform better, yet we couldn't be further from the truth. Self-criticism does not help you develop your self-awareness, research has shown that it is sabotage, disrupting our performance and hurting productivity.

Women tend to fall into this trap and can be highly self-critical, blaming themselves when they fail and crediting their success to others. Men on the other hand, tend to blame circumstances for their failure and credit their wins to themselves.

Self-compassion is critical in developing our resilience; gaining greater perspective and decision making, enabling us to bounce back and learn from our mistakes, lowering stress levels and decreasing the overwhelm. Rather than self-criticism, we need to practice self-compassion. Take notice of 'your negative head talk' and regularly practice reframing negative thoughts with the positive. The power of thinking is extraordinary, and we don't credit it enough. Change your thinking to build your resilience. Resilience teaches us self-awareness which in turn gives us the confidence to fight our fears.

Learning to develop your self-awareness gives you much greater confidence. When your confidence and self-esteem are strengthened, you'll find that you're able to make good decisions. When you learn to become an assertive decision maker, then you're on your way to being self-aware. When you have started to master your self-awareness, you have greater ability to prioritise tasks.

Focused prioritising helps us adapt to different occasions, situations and events. To help you focus, write a 'to-do-list' or a checklist, don't keep it in your head. Writing down tasks prompts your brain to focus clearly and be organised. When you stay on top of your 'to-do-list' you feel a sense of satisfaction that you've achieved, which in turn gives you a sense of control. By mastering **focused prioritising**, you start to become more disciplined in your habits and your existence. You become more finely attuned. Well-disciplined thinking will provide you with a greater ability to cope during tough times. A well-developed sense of self-awareness empowers you to delegate to others with ease. It enables clarity.

Delegation of tasks is both the easiest and hardest thing to do, because it challenges our emotions and our thinking. Understanding the constant tug between head and heart is an important strength that helps us to recognise what we need to do.

Once you've mastered this, you'll develop a **reflective attitude** and without this, you will find that going places becomes a chore. On this journey, you need a reflective attitude. When driving on a long trip, it's vital that you have the necessary gear to get you from A to B. A reliable plan, dependable vehicle, accurate maps and adequate toolbox, to avoid problems that occur along the way. If you aren't a confident person, going on a solo journey may make you feel anxious, overwhelmed and cause procrastination.

Trusting technology is the first step to building your confidence travelling into the unknown. Travel broadens our minds, pressing the reset button in our brains to marvel at what we see around us. A GPS can fail due to off the grid driving and you will be obligated to face your fears and draw on your past experiences and skills to find your way. You will need to communicate effectively and proficiently with others to help you through challenges.

Food and water are essential on any journey and if you choose not to sustain and hydrate correctly, you'll begin to feel tired, grumpy and lack focus. Stop regularly along the way providing your body with the correct nutrition and hydration it requires to stay mentally alert for the trip. Too many people think it's smart to make long distance trips in record time but all they do is contribute to the road toll.

The hardest thing about building resilience is finding the motivation to change our habits; what we think of ourselves, what we eat, how we dress, our attitude, how we commit to regular exercise and the social activities we choose. Our daily activities intersect and overlap with each other, often competing for our attention.

We need motivation to build our resilience. Motivation is the hand that holds the key to courage, that unlocks the door to self-confidence. Unless you're motivated, you will not have the courage to face each day. The door to self-confidence must be wide open and you must be prepared, organised and equipped to start your journey to success.

First, you need to clear away the chatter in your head. The voice that talks you out of doing the things you want to do. Success is a mindset. Avoid thinking about your differences, failings or weaknesses and re-think your strengths and abilities.

Bullying in schools

Working as a state school principal in violent rural schools, I experienced a long, harrowing journey and became a veteran in bullying, harassment, cyber hate, physical assault, paedophiles, trolling, rape, fetishes, suicide and murder. Bullying is prevalent in all schools and I witnessed daily harassment of students against students, students against staff, staff against students, parents against staff and staff against staff. I also witnessed serious bullying of principals by fellow principals, regional and central office staff. Bullying is a pandemic not just in schools and government departments, it's dangerous and contagious proportions in Australia are clearly associated with the **tall poppy syndrome**.

Bullying is mostly silent, other than to the victims. Most bullies hide behind their prestige, positions, computers, phones, buildings or in toilets – people are too scared to say anything because of the repercussions.

One of the things I'm constantly saddened and amazed by, is the *head in sand* attitude by people, government officers and politicians, who just don't want to know about bullying, criminal activity or behaviours. It's all because of **fear**. I would love a dollar for every time since 2010 someone said to me, 'just leave, don't say anything, don't fight them, **they'll get you'.**

'They'll get you' is a standard threat in the kids' playground, a standard threat in the workplace by adults, and standard language across our government departments. Who's going to 'get' who and how are they going to 'get' them? It's an ill-informed threat and misguided opinion believed by so many. A control strategy used by bullies. We see it daily in the schoolyard and workplaces.

When I arrived at my first high school, I was immediately instructed by the admin staff how things were to run in their school and by whom. The tall poppy syndrome was alive and well and the school was run by the admin staff, none of whom were trained in education, but all were self-appointed educators.

When I arrived, the school buildings, classrooms and grounds were filthy and battered. Every single wall internally, externally and ceilings had holes punched in them. Inside the computer lab, exposed wires hung from the roof, the carpet was threadbare and computers broken. One science lab had exposed asbestos and wiring. It was rated on the front page of the Courier Mail as one of the ten worst schools in the state. Where do you start when the budget has no money? The school was so broke that it couldn't even afford to purchase a photocopier. We went for almost a year before we could purchase a second-hand one with zero help from the department.

The school was in total chaos; staff, students and parents. Prior to my arrival, a student had been suspended for holding a girl down on the oval as he burnt her with a lit cigarette. My brief was to clean it up. I was informed that a large sum of money had disappeared from the admin office prior to my arrival and a claim of who took it. No evidence, just an opinion by the self-appointed school leader!

There was no security in the front office. Doors open, staff sat on desks, more interested in selling footy tickets and gossiping about each other than working. My first job was to 'clean up the front office' and my fate was sealed from that day on. They didn't want to work, they wanted to get paid to socialise and bully staff. I came along and disrupted the scheme of things, ruining their social life and fun. Who was I to run their school? Nope, they weren't having a bar of it.

The backlash was real. One employee wrote to the Premier, they weren't going to be told what to do. They reported that I wasn't teaching English in the school! The naive Premier wasted vast taxpayer's dollars with an unnecessary investigation all in the name of appeasing voters, endorsing that person with the immense power to continue antagonising me. This was the first inkling I got that politics in this school played a disturbing role. The lead whinger decided to write two diaries of allegations against me but forgot to cross-check them. I pointed it out to ESU; they hadn't bothered to check. The admin officer had committed a serious offence, blatantly submitting false evidence against me, this is called libel. No reprimand but instead, a promotion. Executive regional officers also knowingly made false and vexatious allegations against me. Once again, nothing happened, but they all received promotions.

Many people made false and malicious allegations against me, without fear, because they were not forced to sign a Statutory Declaration. When I provided the correct information, there was no consequence for these people who had committed libel. In fact, they were rewarded with promotions and a letter, congratulating them on their allegations. Still to this day, they do not know the correct information that their allegations were overturned by me. But I do. What this means is that the Qld department of education supports and promotes corruption under the PSA. So, when these people get on their high horse and whinge and whine about my book, they'll get a nasty surprise and so will the department – because they enjoyed the power of corruption for a decade. I did notify the department of this, but they didn't take me seriously and they don't talk to each other. The pattern of corrupt practices is noticeable, there are countless examples and I have cogent evidence.

The PSA should be reviewed urgently and every person required to sign a Statutory Declaration, if they commit to allegations against another. Government departments would see a huge reduction in investigations when complainants know that others can take legal action against them for libel. This would save the tax payer a shit load of money, especially given that my investigation cost millions due to lack of evidence compelling them to manipulate and bully people, into making false allegations against me to save face and the cost of the large number of promotions to those that assisted them.

The Tall Poppy Syndrome in Australia

The **tall poppy syndrome** describes characteristics of a culture where people of high rank or position are resented, condemned, criticised and cut down because they're considered 'superior' to their peers. The **tall poppy syndrome** phrase can be traced back as early as 1864 in Australia and the term experienced a revival with the publication of Susan Mitchell's best-selling book *Tall Poppies* in 1984 in which Mitchell interviewed nine successful Australian women.

Sociologist Max Weber believes the term *a zero-sum game*, refers to certain social groups and that the achievement of prestige and power provides a rationalisation for the hatred of 'tall poppies'. Weber notes there is only a limited amount of prestige in these groups for its members to share, a minimal quantity of attention, authority and material resources that its members can give to each other. He explains that for someone to rise in status, another person must fall.

In Weber's world, someone who suddenly rises is an absolute threat to everyone else in the group's status. Weber advises that **humiliating or sabotaging** a popular member of the group will lower that person's status and therefore make it possible for the antagonist to replace them in the group's hierarchy. This is what happened to my colleague down the road and I; both females in an archaic male-dominated town, who did not welcome the role of 'women in power' and employed by an equally male dominated archaic and corrupt organisation.

Weber's 'zero-sum pattern' is evident in small rural towns managed by fixed hierarchies where there is little movement in or out of the group. The schoolyard at a micro-level and the school itself, are prime examples of the 'zero-sum pattern'. This explains the Queensland state education department's leadership model, filled from the inside with public servants and teachers on promotion who have little if any understanding, knowledge or external experience running such an enormous government organisation. https://en.wikipedia.org/wiki/Tall poppy syndrome

As a senior female high school principal, I experienced first-hand the wrath of the **tall poppy syndrome**, which grew at an alarming rate. I witnessed bullying behaviours against a number of my female colleagues. The one I remember the most was a principal who was and still is undoubtedly one of the best principals I've ever had the pleasure working with; powerful curriculum content knowledge, great student and staff rapport, kind and caring. They were slaughtered, not just by the parents, but hammered unmercifully by vicious and notoriously nasty colleagues who were relentless, not stopping until that principal was removed. I reported their corrupt behaviours to the CCC. Glowing with their success, they started on me.

Be FEARless

If you have reached this point, then you're willing and ready to start on a road less travelled – an exciting new journey in building motivation and developing your resilience.

We tend to live mainly within our conscious selves. The emotions and instincts that drive us are outside our bodies because we live such busy lives. Unless we can learn to focus on **ourselves** successfully and become motivated, we won't become courageous. Courage unlocks the car door so we can start the engine and take control of our journey to becoming resilient.

Strap on your seatbelt, start the engine and take control of your life! Welcome to your new journey.

End of Chapter Activity

Write a Journal

Write in a journal every night before you go to bed.

Write down three things you do well.

This helps you to target your focus on small wins, which will help build your self-confidence.

By journaling in this way, you are developing your resilience for the difficult times - allowing yourself permission to accept your strengths and appreciate them.

CHAPTER THREE

Calibrate your GPS

Our internal GPS is our own personal compass that controls the balance in our ability to cope with change, grow our resilience and improve our self-confidence. When that balance is altered then we need to recalibrate it. Our lives are permanently in a state of change and our internal GPS is the tool that we use to modify the balance that is necessary in a positive way; to help us grow, achieve and succeed. When we calibrate our internal GPS, we're regulating our attitudes and tuning our self-awareness to adapt to change.

This chapter is about how to change your thinking and attitudes, by calibrating your GPS. For many of us, when we look in the mirror at our reflection, we initially see ourselves as the person we wish to be. But if you wait long enough, your true image starts to become clearer, much like digital photo pixelating.

Our absorbent culture of 'selfies' in the cyber world masks the reality of our lives to the viewer and very possibly to ourselves. Social media photos portray how we want to be perceived by the public, leading us to question - is it authentic? Is it really you? Photos are one snapshot in time that disguise the real you and hide the challenges and frustrations that surround us in our daily lives.

Suffering the loss of a close family member, friend, marriage, job or trauma can cause many significant impacts on our daily lives. When faced with adversity, our potential to function to our maximum ability is determined by our levels of resilience.

Our capacity to recover is dependent on several circumstances, some within our reach and others well beyond our reach. The range of difficulty of these circumstances affects our recovery, which results in how quickly we can adjust towards how we approach change or how quickly we deteriorate because we cannot alter our thinking to adapt to change. Recovery from depression, unhappiness or opposition is largely influenced by the flexibility of our own levels of resilience.

When we use our internal GPS to recalibrate our attitudes, actions, emotions and behaviours, the fog then begins to lift and the windscreen in time becomes clearer. Our clarity changes from low to high visibility, enabling us to see clearly where we are headed in our journey. It is only then that we become motivated to continually alter and readjust our internal GPS for maximum precision and focus.

Change

Change is a major factor in our personal and professional lives. With each subsequent change, people start struggling; becoming isolated and lonely, entering a downhill spiral of cognitive functioning which starts to affect the way we think and operate in our daily lives. This includes reduced problem-solving, diminished decision making and fear of the unknown. Subsequently, our outlook on life becomes faded, causing a further decline in thinking and making our ability to remain positive difficult.

Many people resist change because it makes their life seem more difficult. The only barrier you have against coping with change, is yourself. Most of us find change a challenge but we can deal with it by learning to recalibrate our internal GPS.

There are many 'potholes in the road' to challenge you. Some people are not able to cope due to their lack of resilience, so we need to reverse out of the garage and take a trip somewhere new. If we leave the highway occasionally and take the road less travelled, we discover that the risk is rewarding. We experience the buzz of achievement that is a result of conquering our fears, we increase our experiences by rehearsing 'feeling the fear'. We need to look outside our comfort zone and retrain our old thinking. Too often we inherit so much of our thinking from our parents or those that influence us the most, that the lens of our reflection is smeared, and we find it extremely difficult to see clearly.

Our close family members are committed to helping us and try to do this by making us do things their way. This can cause great resistance because we begin to rebel against the 'old traditional ways'. The result is that we rapidly learn to practice external control of that situation. Most importantly is what we **don't learn** and that's the underlying motivation for our behaviours.

As adults, we resist because we have grown up being taught how to take care of ourselves as was intended by our parents, caregivers, teachers and friends. Ultimately, we learned to become independent.

What is the underlying motivation for these behaviours? Why do some of us rebel and others don't? Why do some adult children get treated as adolescents by their parents? One very important thing I have learned in life is that no matter how old my mother is, she continually watches her middle-aged children for signs of improvement! My father did this too, he was convinced that I would grow up one day but never granted me the keys to his ride-on lawnmower!

We swiftly learn the practice of controlling others when we're born. Our constant demands for food, comfort, warmth and attention are instantly met by our nurturers who're predominantly our mothers. It becomes a practice which feeds our needy, controlling behaviours. As we grow older, we learn to take care of ourselves and in time, we learn to take care of others who cross into our lives. We're a nation of people who generously care for others that we don't know. We donate to charities run by people we don't know. We are easily scammed on the internet by those who don't care but see our strong desire to help others as a weakness they can exploit. Some of us are easily cheated by those who are adept in the art of swindling our emotions and money.

To learn to change, we must learn how to care for ourselves first and foremost. If we are to become resilient then we need to know

Calibrate your GPS

how to take care of ourselves. We need to develop our ability to reflect across several areas; health, fitness and mindset; these three areas are vital to growing stronger in our self-belief.

When we start to pay attention to these areas, then we begin to focus on our ability to problem-solve, which builds our resilience and coping mechanisms.

If you want the power to influence your own life, then you must learn the skills needed to build your resilience. If you aren't where you want to be in life, that should be enough motivation for you to make changes to your attitude. Give yourself permission to accept your failures … you will learn how to be brave, fearless and not give a shit!

There are many 'pot-holes in the road', tasks, encounters and challenges that we find distressing, difficult and at times bloody painful. When you get stuck in a boggy pothole, you can be guaranteed that you will not get out unless you learn to change your thinking and develop some problem-solving skills very quickly. When you have become skilled in problem-solving, then you will master the ability to adapt to change.

Adapting to change empowers us with confidence. We need to learn to let go of external control, we are driven by power. It's the desire for power that overtakes survival early in our lives as we grow into adults and directs us in the way we choose to live. Many of us who like chocolate would readily admit that after we open that beautifully wrapped box and smell the aromas of those sweet delicacies, we know when we've eaten our fill. So why is it that we still want more, and the pleasure associated with that, means others get less? This behaviour obstructs our ability to share and way too often I've heard the same old story of long-term relationships that have ended because someone in the partnership is consumed with the need for more.

The quest for this feeling of power is in our government departments. We see it in the structure of these organisations; top-heavy with an excess of senior officials paying homage to each other in an unhealthy, godlike way, expecting others to follow suit, thereby preserving the hold on their own power.

This pursuit of power is insatiable, and some officials and politicians have no misgivings about doing whatever they desire, to gain or maintain power at any cost. Power is linked to politics, plenty of political parties and government departments have been and continue to be destroyed this way, along with the integrity of our nation, now more than ever before.

We see it daily on TV and social media, political parties jostling for power using petty personal attacks against each other, to gain attention, just like bullying school children. Rather than doing what they're elected and paid to do - help their country to grow up - they prefer the ease of blowing wind against each other and causing drama to distract voters to what they're not doing. Australia is not growing up and will continue until every party changes their attitude, mode of operation, behaviours and adopts society-friendly communications. The pleasure associated with the perception of 'having power' means that some will sacrifice a marriage, relationship, destroy a colleague, business competitor, assault, steal, murder or rape a child. Why? Because it's inherent, the need for power starts when we're born.

Change is necessary and it's achievable. The need for freedom is the balance to the need for power. External control rules over power and is the opponent of freedom. That stability continues to rock perilously at every level all over the world.

I read an example of this in a local paper, a sickening article about a refugee who'd raped a four-year-old girl and a judge who ruled 'no discipline' against the rapist denying the federal police application to deport him back to his country, because he'd had a tough life back home. The only discipline the convicted rapist received was keeping his refugee status, rather than be granted Australian Citizenship. He was rewarded with the highest level of freedom that we hold so dear in this country and set free to roam the streets again, to possibly rape more innocent and vulnerable, pre-school girls. The power that judge owned was self-serving, rather than truly ethical.

Change is about becoming creative in our problem-solving abilities. We create the ability to exceed or destruct; life's scales tip from happy to unhappy, angry to calm, fulfilled to overwhelmed, full to empty. Our mind dictates how we think, feel and act, so if we want to change anything in our lives, we must exercise the mind as if it were a muscle. Using the brain makes it stronger and it behaves like a muscle. This is where you go 'cold turkey' and just do it! This is where you decide to stop smoking or drinking that 3rd glass of wine with dinner.

Our brain can be trained to improve different intellectual functions. The first step towards muscular contraction is the signal from the brain instructing it to contract. This is where the mind meets the body and it's known as the **neuromuscular junction**. Studies have shown that we can exercise our brain and protect it from shrinking as it ages. Research has revealed that keeping fit with exercise can increase **neurogenesis,** or the formation of new brain cells. You can also exercise your brain with puzzles, card games, brain games, and board games. To learn more on this topic, research the above words on the internet, typed in bold.

Keeping your brain in shape is the key to building strong resilience. Build your mental strength and awareness by creating a strong mindset, balancing your emotions with reason, distinguishing between procrastination and problem-solving and following your own advice!

What is change? It's about making the future course of your life different from what it is currently. If you're reading this book, then you are more than able to make change for yourself. If you can change your attitude to one that improves your life, then you will become more confident. If you gain greater self-confidence, then you will begin to build your resilience. The actions and consequences are like that of an athlete training to improve their PB (personal best).

Goal Setting – *WHAT? Goals*

To achieve your vision, you need goals and to develop your goals effectively, you need the blueprint for my **'WHAT? Goals'**.

Our daily activities intersect and overlap with each other, resulting in increased competition for our attention. When we create a vision for ourselves, we usually look at what is currently happening. We create our visualisation with our eyes wide open, pulling ideas from what is already occurring, in the hope that we can improve our lives. We think this works, because it's safe.

Calibrate your GPS

"Begin by clearing away the chatter in your head that makes you talk yourself out of doing the things that you want to do."
Tracy Tully

If we truly change our course in life, we would need to recalculate our direction much like a GPS does, and find another route. This appears to be a much more extreme way to create a picture for ourselves, so we should be doing it with our eyes firmly shut.

If we draw inspiration from within us, rather than from outside of us, then we'd be dreaming of things that we never thought possible. As a woman living in rural, remote and isolated areas, I needed to constantly review my attitudes, to help me to adapt and diversify, to survive the tyranny of working in a male-dominated and aggressively violent world.

Too often, we reject the voice in our head and instead, we listen to the voices of others, believing their opinions to be much more credible than those of our own. We do this because it's safer.

To develop a new dream, we need to breathe life into our inside voice. We must follow our own path, not the path that the loudest voice outside tells us to follow. The only way we can do this is to give the dream inside our head a name. Give that dream permission to play and turn it up loud, put it on auto-repeat and play it repeatedly until it sounds normal. Turn up the volume; the louder the vision, the easier it is to accomplish.

Once our vision becomes 'normal' in our thoughts, the receptors in our brain recognise it and stop resisting it. The human 'fight or flight' response is our instinct that naturally controls our brain and our rhythm of life. Our brain then learns to feel comfortable following our dream. We have broken a habit and formed a ritual that allows routines and goals to develop. **That is what makes us more resilient.**

When we have a convincing dream, it becomes a vision complete with a solid foundation and articulated with confidence, then the rest will follow. Others will 'get it'. There will be less resistance because you're in control and in effect, educating others.

Too often, we're hoodwinked into thinking that if we aim small, then we'll achieve our goals, but the opposite is true. A strong vision is genuine and with the right team behind it, will strengthen no matter who you are, where you go or where you are.

Painting an image of a future vision that exceeds what people are familiar with, will have visible effects on others. Those who are not ambitious will be the 'don't go for it' group and those who are motivated, will be optimistic for **your** success and will tell you 'go for it'!

Beware of the pessimists, those are the nay-sayers, the knockers and the negative Nancies, who quite frankly don't understand you or your vision and don't want to. They want you to stay exactly where you are, because that is where they are, in a safe place. Remember that learned behaviour of control? That's an example in action, you've seen it!

Most people need to be led. Very few people are natural leaders, know how to lead or are even inclined to lead. In my lifetime, I have met few natural and strong leaders; they are extremely rare.

Calibrate your GPS

"My creed is 'seeking sensations', when the reward far outweighs the risks."

Tracy Tully

The **WHAT? Goals** theory was developed by me for my online programmes and you'll find it on my website **www.tracytully.com**

It's intended to help individuals make appropriate choices and learn improved problem-solving and decision-making skills.

WHAT? Goals is a self-help model that assists people to reduce their anxiety around managing information by providing a clear plan for monitoring their self-progress.

End of Chapter Activity

WHAT? Goals

W – <u>what</u> do you want to change?
H – <u>how</u> will you do it?
A – <u>achieve</u> with small steps
T – <u>time</u> it will take

This 4-step model can be used in simple activities or for much more complex tasks. The following example is one I've used. It's suitable for anyone who wishes to drop weight. My weight loss target was 10 kilograms. I didn't have any choice in the matter. It was an instruction from my GP so my blood pressure would return to normal and I could continue my life with premium health.

Apply my model to your situation by following my example below, making sure that you keep it short, simple and achievable for your individual capabilities:

W – What - lose 10 kg in 6 months

H – How
- adopt 5 morning Micro Habits
- purchase book "What the Fat?"
- book two private Pilates lessons per week
- perform daily exercises - stretching, squats and lifting arm weights
- eat appropriate food as advised by my doctor
- increase my daily water uptake
- don't shop when I'm hungry
- clean out fridge and pantry of 'fat' food

- make a lunch box for work every day
- eat small healthy meals regularly, decrease carbohydrates
- go to the beach and wear a bikini

A – Achieve
- attend two Pilates classes per week coached 1:1
- increase arm weights 1kg to 3 kg after first fortnight
- increase five arm lifts/day every week by 5
- perform daily stretching and lifting exercises
- photograph body improvement of muscle definition every month
- take measurements of key body parts every month
- eat for performance not for comfort
- record my daily nutrition and fitness on mobile app
- monitor weekly nutrition and exercise data in my diary
- weigh myself on scales first Monday morning of every month
- buy a new swimsuit

T – TIME – I will achieve this in 6 months with the reward of a holiday to my favourite destination

When a simple model such as the four-step **WHAT?** *Goals* model is broken down into a short and succinct plan, like the one I developed to lose weight, we find that our historically poor reasoning or cognitive functioning, reduced problem-solving, and diminished decision-making, is improved.

When a goal is achieved, the changed behaviours are rewarded; the spiral progresses steadily upwards, becoming a positive one. You can continue to face greater challenges by applying this mode for each new situation. You will see that I have intentionally rewarded myself with both physical and non-physical booty for my efforts;

important psychologically as a reward for good behaviour which creates a feeling of contentment and achievement.

Remember the external power of control you learned about early in this chapter? Now you are using it for good and the glass is half full, not half empty!

CHAPTER FOUR

Maintenance

"You don't have to be someone special to achieve something amazing. You've just got to have a dream, believe in it and work hard."

Jessica Watson

It's critically important to conduct regular maintenance checks on your vehicle before you start a long journey. The essentials you can see at a glance; tyres, lights, indicators, windscreen, fuel, radiator and oil; the basics capable of being checked by any driver. Book your car into a mechanic before commencing on a long trip, don't leave it until after you've broken down in an isolated place.

Why do we look after our cars better than we look after ourselves? Self-maintenance is just as critical on a long journey. The car gets us from A to B, but it's the person in charge of the vehicle that ultimately holds all the responsibility for the safety of not only their passengers, but everyone on the roads around them.

Justin Herald believes that people choose to neglect themselves because they place more emphasis on material things, our attitude towards life determining what life doles back to us, the old cause and effect rule. Attitude is something we can control; it's a choice. Most of us never really take note of our own attitude regularly. We adjust our attitude when we wake up in accordance with our morning routine and tweak it as the day goes on according to our moods, letting our circumstances rule our lives.

For Herald, attitude is one of the first things we need to check when we get up in the morning. He refers to it as 'the accelerator pedal on our lives' and just like the accelerator in our cars, it determines the pace of our lives.
https://epdf.tips/would-you-like-attitude-with-that-no-limits-no-excuses-no-ifs-no-buts-just-attitude

I've found in the workforce time and again, especially in rural, remote and violent schools, that employees who are unhappy with their lives always dump their negativity on everyone else, who become equally miserable. This is prevalent in staffrooms; the group then becomes even more unhappy, feeding off each other's gloom and it spreads like fire.

I've also found in those circumstances that if you love life, want the best out of life and project that attitude, there will be some that will choose to respond positively. Such is the power of negativity. Positive people build us up wanting the best for us. My last boss told me I was too happy - really? Poor leadership, zero mentoring,

Maintenance

data driven, all in a 30 minute once a term visit. It's no wonder our region was the worst in the state.

Until you change your attitude, nothing changes around you. It's no good waiting for people around you to change, they won't - they enjoy living with doom and gloom and invite it into their lives. These people are drama kings and queens, thriving on living the life of a victim.

It's your life, your dreams and your goals; you are the driver of your own destiny. It just depends where you want to steer your car and whether you want to take the road well-travelled or like me, the road less travelled.

The essential gear in your **WHAT? Goals TOOLBOX** will help you learn how to change your habits if you know how to use them correctly. The tools build your resilience, so It's time to take a good look at yourself; look in the mirror and have a good close look at your reflection. This is the snapshot picture others get of you. In three seconds, they appraise you. That instant snap in a three-second time slot says everything about you and simultaneously, nothing at all.

If you want to project a good image, this is the first point to check because it's the point where others use their observation to gauge you. It's very important to stay attuned to how you project, and I don't mean by keeping up with those who are wearing the best labels, touting the latest plastic surgery or driving the most expensive car.

"For every action, there is a corresponding and equal reaction."
Anonymous

The term 'resilient' can have many definitions, such as: flexible, hardy, quick to recover, strong and tough (*Collins Thesaurus*) so I guess that shearers and pole dancers are really resilient! In this chapter, I focus on self-maintenance and building stronger resilience. Together we'll travel on a new highway and work towards becoming more self-confident through our resilience. This book tugs harder at the strings of every woman who picks it up; it's a book to draw strength from.

On my free website www.mrwcoaching.com, I seek to empower others to confront their weaknesses and assist feelings of helplessness, by providing a purely non-marketing and sales website with supporting articles, blogs and an opportunity for readers to contribute their stories in an effort to support and inspire others. My business website www.tracytully.com offers online programmes, public speaking events, workshops, retreats and a unique 1:1 consultation; *'Finding Your Sweet Spot'*. I have a deep understanding of the strength that people need today to build their resilience to face challenges in life for tomorrow. We all need psychological strength to build resilience as well as physical strength for fitness.

The hardest thing about building resilience is to find the motivation to change our habits. The only person who controls our behaviour is us. In the workplace, if we're made to feel exposed using reprimand for poor performance statistics that are out of our control, we begin to feel uninspired to do well. If the process of intimidation is repeated regularly, then we develop resistance and this is when we begin to feel the need to change the situation. I experienced this repeatedly as a principal and the expectation of my leaders was for me to emulate it, it was a no-win situation and state achievement results demonstrate it.

When we realise that our behaviour is only controlled by ourselves and not others, then we start to reinterpret our sense of personal freedom, discovering swiftly that we have way more freedom than we ever thought. It's then that we change how we think and realise that we can choose how much freedom we're willing to give up to make changes to the situation.

We need **motivation** to build our resilience. Motivation is the hand that holds the key of **courage** that unlocks the door to **self-confidence**. Unless we're motivated, we won't have the courage to face each day unless the door to self-confidence is wide open.

In the previous chapter, we discovered that as babies, we learned to use external control. As adults, some use external control to gain power, whether in a good or bad way. The person who agitated against me to procure my job used external control to gain power over me with a leader who they had a close connection and control with. We know that individuals have the power to affect the lives of others, and in some cases, this influence is malicious.

The power of the human spirit

Despite dreadful examples of manipulation and control, the human spirit can soar far beyond the power of those who want to control it. A great example of this happened to me when one of my perpetrators manipulated others to 'falsify allegations' against me prior to, during and following my investigation. After I tabled my evidence to the Director-General and the CCC, the perpetrator disappeared.

A principal contacted me advising that the ESU had arrived on their doorstep to interview, attempting to manipulate them into making false allegations about me. They were quite fearful of the ESU's confrontational way they conducted their interview. When they weren't successful in obtaining an allegation against me, in a desperate effort to tarnish me, their last question was, 'What didn't you like about her?' This was a standard question they used with everyone, evident in interview transcripts, highlighting the fact they had no evidence, leaving them with the only option they had, to forcefully procure false allegations against me.

Many others spoke to me with similar stories. At the end of my investigation, the department sent a letter thanking the principal for their allegations against me. The principal was livid, demanding an apology, which they received. A copy of both letters were passed to me; cogent evidence of libel, clearly demonstrating department culture, manipulative and corrupt behaviours. Recently, just prior to going to print, I was privy to similar correspondence detailing once again, corrupt behaviours and actions by ESU.

Mother's Day 10th May 2020, the Courier Mail published a front-page article "Premier loses the Treasurer to integrity scandal during worst economic hit in nearly a century". Labor Party Deputy Premier Jackie Tradd's alleged political interference, with the appointment of an independent public service panel process. Tracey Cook the new Inner-City South State Secondary College Principal had her appointment cancelled in private meetings held with Regional Director Greg Hunt, in favour of preferred principal, Kirsten Ferdinands. The school in Tradd's electorate, with Hunt and Tradd stood down by the CCC under investigation. Despite public service selection processes protected by law, I have evidence of a similar case, conducted in the DD&SW Region. In fact, there have been many 'special' promotions of individuals in this region and a lot of them happened in conjunction with my stand down.

Maintenance

I'm privy to the history of some of those underbelly dealings in their earliest days.

Power is never simply confined to established or recognised authority. It also operates in the underbelly of society and that underbelly can be as close as your state government education department.

> *"There is a point where you go beyond resilience to resistance, it's there that I refuse to retreat."*
>
> **Tracy Tully**

Calibrating your internal GPS ensures that you have the balance required to use your power for optimum improvement in your own life and not others. How can you change your views, thinking and actions, to get them back on track towards achieving your goals? Goals that you planned years ago. Dreams that you wished to become reality.

It's not whether you get knocked down ... its whether you get back up. It's a hard slog, with many disappointments as well as successes. We must strive to be better and try to reach new experiences. We all go through life wanting more, the problem is, many of us fall short and become disillusioned with our goals and dreams. We may even give up entirely and stop applying ourselves to achieve what we set out to do.

There's no difference between you and me. Anyone who elevates themselves over others is only cheating themselves and those around them and they become cold and timid, never experiencing the exhilaration of achievement or torment of failure.

If nothing changes, then nothing happens. Don't fear change. Most times, change will bring about a welcome release, eventually. Use your frustration with where life is at and where it is headed and channel that frustration towards a permanent change in your own life, not others.

Fear of failure stops us trying many new things in life. Many people fear change and are resistant to any sort of change in their lives, even something as simple as changing their toothpaste or deodorant. We're all creatures of habit. Failure may be the road to success, but you won't know unless you try it.

Are you sick and tired of facing the same situations, the same frustrations every day, week and year? Then you need to take charge of your life and show yourself what you can do by changing your thinking and actions. If you believe, then you will succeed. Driving to and from work every day using the same route? You can be sure that at some stage, you will become complacent, lose your concentration and start to lose focus on the road in front of you.

Look around you at your workmates, friends and family. How many are living their dreams and have reached their prized life? The answer will be not many. Just remember, successful people don't complain about lack of opportunities. Those opportunities are right under your nose and are usually the opportunities you overlook because you chose not to see.

The surest sign that a person is successful in their job, is when they say, 'It's the best job in the world!' The secret to achievement is to keep chipping away at a task which once seemed too much for you. You will achieve that by breaking tasks into bite-sized chunks.

Maintenance

Only a person who has conquered their own faults is properly qualified to be a leader of others. The person who can't guide themselves is no guide for others. It's in a storm that you'll learn who the best driver is. It's the one who has patience because they understand that everything is difficult before it becomes easy. Whoever said that the road is smooth?

If we look at difficulties as opportunities, then the person who overcomes them builds resilience. They accept a challenge because they're not afraid of failure and are skilled at problem-solving because their attitude to difficult tasks is to keep working at it. They're not afraid to share their ideas and solutions with others at a cognitive functioning level like their own. Like-minded people seek out like-minded people.

Which road do you take? If you read the signs along the road, then you will learn from the lessons. The decisions you make will take you to the correct turn at the intersection, instead of the one that is either going nowhere or in the wrong direction to where you want to go. Each town on your trip you reach, is equivalent to a goal achieved.

You may have tried to reach those goals, but due to unforeseen circumstances, you have fallen short in your estimation of the fuel needed along the way. A semi-truck takes out a road sign on a corner – someone's actions result in you going backwards. You have been let down by those you thought had your best interests at heart. We all have. Along the way you've called a friend for directions, but you know that you should have been better prepared and researched the road before starting on your trip. What you learn from those experiences will ultimately be the key to pushing you through those mental barriers and that is resilience.

The things we like to do are never difficult to accomplish. When you're travelling on an adventure, don't choose the easiest road, but instead, choose the best. It will become easier after a while. Positive people don't wait for opportunities to come knocking on their door, they go looking for them. Too often, people fail to do things to help themselves because they believe that opportunities will come to them. I've seen way too many waiting for that perfect job to be handed to them on a plate.

Passion

The feeling of passion can turn into action. Why are some people successful? The answer is simple; they've mastered one factor in reaching their goals – using their passion, they find their sweet spot!

We need to use our passion to follow our dreams. Passion is why we do what we do and how well we enjoy it. Everyone can achieve, it's how well and how passionately you do it that relates to how great the rewards are at the end. I have learned the hard way; never let your emotions rule your decisions in your business or life.

Attitude

Our attitude is the actions and feelings that determine our life goals. If you have a negative approach to your life, then your outcome will be negative. The simple 'cause and effect' rule. Have you ever sat and watched children learning to swim? They don't think of the past or the future, they enjoy the present, which very few adults do with intent.

Maintenance

Every road we travel has a bend. If you don't take the bend, you will veer off onto another track and then you'll find that you're not going in the right direction. So, how can you begin to help yourself? Surround yourself with passionate, positive, big thinkers. Their vision are infectious and you'll find you're drawn to them and caught up in their mood.

It's said you can change a bad habit over a period of 30 days. For example, losing weight and exercising daily. You'll be inspired to find the motivation to target your habits for resilience by getting off your butt and having a go.

End of Chapter Activity

Take a good look at yourself and using your impartial lens as your attitude tool, examine the following:

- what do you think of yourself?
- how do you eat?
- how do you dress?
- how do you wear your hair?
- how do you commit to exercise?
- what social activities do you choose?

Self-maintenance requires a sassy attitude to jump in your car and go!

We tend to live mainly with our conscious selves. The emotions and instincts that drive us are outside our bodies because we live such busy lives. Unless you can learn to focus on yourself successfully, you cannot start the journey to becoming resilient.

"Seek sensations, the reward far outweighs the risk."
Tracy Tully

CHAPTER FIVE

Start the Engine

"Turn off the safety switch and take charge of your insecurities."

Tracy Tully

Motivation is the steering wheel for your resilience. You drive your resilience through your determined motivation. Both terms go hand in hand. Just like *Jack and Jill,* both hands need to be holding the pail of water.

A person who worked for me years ago experienced great joy in describing me as 'eccentric', which I found curiously interesting. They chose this word as a passive 'put down', consciously choosing the power of words with the intent to make me feel inadequate and destabilise my self-worth. I was aware they wanted my job.

> *"What makes you different or weird – that's your strength."*
> **Meryl Streep**

That person was notorious for their bitterness, regularly spewing vitriol on anyone they cornered. They failed to comprehend that I'm an observer and the psychology of behaviour fascinates me and having years of their self-destructive behaviour. I simply tuned out. Not only were they slow to pick up on the fact that I wasn't listening, but also didn't understand that the entire staff were regularly complaining about them.

They were avoiding work and only did just enough to fly under the radar. Not a team player, arguing with everyone, a pessimist, slinking around the work site wreaking negative havoc on all. They were toxic. Every worksite has one. Sadly, they became the most despised person, but didn't see it, they needed to develop their self-awareness and become the person they were truly capable of being.

> *"Everything we hear is an opinion, not a fact.*
> *Everything we see is a perspective, not the truth".*
> **Marcus Aurelius**

By putting me down to others, they elected to boost themselves up. Bullying in the workplace is an example of how others will drag you down to focus on themselves, believing it makes them look good. Sadly, they're deceiving themselves.

For many years as a principal, whilst I had the immense fortune of working with some amazing, hard-working people, too often I found myself running an adult day-care centre for a group of people who would not take control of their own lives and were hell-bent on controlling others. Throwing toddler tantrums to redirect their inadequacies away from them and onto me, they didn't want to do any of the hard work, but they wanted the pay. Sadly, they will never change and never grow. Sound familiar?

Remember, selfish people don't care about you, unless you're doing something for them, and you learn a lot about people when they don't get what they want. Ungrateful people always complain about the things you haven't done for them and show no thanks for the hundreds of things you have done for them. Don't invest your precious time on people who are toxic and who think it's your obligation to provide them with a wonderful and successful life!

> *"I don't like to call it revenge ... returning the favour sounds nicer."*
> **Anonymous**

It's a great story because that person helped me become stronger and more resilient. I could see clearly through my bullshit lens. Unfortunately, that person took great pleasure ensuring the demise of others and was insidious and spiteful, which made me understand just how lonely and sad they were. This person's presence in my life taught me a strong lesson; firstly, rid your life of toxic people quickly and secondly, don't feel sorry for them as they'll never change. Always remember, if you try to keep everyone happy, the person who won't be happy is you.

Working in such a highly volatile world was a real 'dog eat dog' culture and every day my staff and I were on the end of constant verbal abuse. It was an environment that police officers, paramedics, doctors and prison officers experience. It becomes tiring after a while and I eventually developed a desensitised attitude. Ranters, ravers and standover merchants have been around for centuries. But when I listened to playback recordings and paid attention to what these angry people were saying, it was clear that they couldn't cope with life or work. I was just the vessel they spewed their vile vomit at. I was their unpaid counsellor!

> "I walk around like everything is fine, but deep down, inside my shoe, my sock is sliding off."
>
> **Anonymous**

When I posted the above quote on Facebook, one of my followers replied with such a great line that I asked if I could share it in this book:

> "Worry not, I feel the same but let's keep walking, only the foot understands where the shoes pinches."
>
> **Jessy Mack**

Gaining strength from adversity

For my entire life, I've heard the saying, 'what doesn't kill us makes us stronger'. It's so true! When we suffer from major adversity, we chose to either succumb to stress or we choose to understand that we can follow the route to post-traumatic growth. Buddhists believe in the transformative power of understanding; we must motivate ourselves to have the capacity to understand it. So, how do we grow out of a distressing event?

FEARless is a book that shares life after a trauma and difficult situation. If you want to live your passion in a way that makes you happy, you need to learn to rise above challenges. Throughout this book, you will read that choosing to respond to challenges instead of letting them frustrate you, requires focus on your habits and behaviours.

On arrival at one of my schools, I found many classroom teachers had been in their profession for over two decades. They taught students the same way for 20 years, using the systems and methods they learned in college and the teaching practices and behaviour methods of those recommended by their bosses over the decades. These staff failed to change as the organisational system changed over the years and rejoiced working in a little pocket protected from the world of change. The trouble was, their techniques weren't working, and the academic data and behaviour levels of the students clearly demonstrated this.

I found I was in a school predominantly run by the 'should' method, with the older staff fiercely clinging to their outdated processes and methods because 'it should work'. And they got the same results as everyone else who used the 'it should work' method – causing them to become bitter and frustrated with 'the system'. The younger staff were irritated, causing frustration across the school.

Here's a common example; a student won't do their work in class and disrupts others who want to work. The teacher keeps them in during lunch, rings the parents, sends notes home and still the student won't work and continues not being interested in class. The teacher becomes frustrated, so they keep them in at lunchtime again, ring parents, send notes home. The student still doesn't participate in class and the teacher becomes more frustrated. The cycle continues to build until the final level is suspension from school. This causes frustration with the parents and the regional office because they don't want to field the complaints. The teacher rejected changing their methods and the content of their lessons and blamed the student for the problem.

High-performing teachers always go one step further. When faced with a challenging student, they look at what they've done, gauge whether it's working and adjust it. If that doesn't work, they try something else. They keep trying new solutions until they find the one that works. 'Should' teachers don't do this, they avoid the work required to overcome the challenging students and won't change because they don't want to.

High-performing teachers take risks and the main difference between winners and losers is that **winners lose more often than losers.** Winners also win far more and that's because they don't get frustrated, give up and start the 'blame game'. High-performing teachers use the negative data and observation as stepping-stones towards building achievement. Those are the staff members who have their eye on the goal all the time and are willing to accept a setback if it helps them to achieve success. High-performing teachers look for creative solutions to problems and will keep adapting and adjusting to difficult challenges.

Until my arrival at this school, the older teachers managed to fly under the radar. When I directed the change in accordance with department requirements, I swiftly became the object for blame; which was good for the students because it gave them a rest for a while! The 'should' method stayed in place. The more they resisted our department's requirements, the more they blamed me. They continued with their 'should' methods until their frustration was so high that they complained about me to the union. They failed to see that they were part of the problem and my boss told me that everyone supports a loud whinger in our department - no kidding! They became unhappy and passed the hot potato of unhappiness back and forth to each other, building the momentum of blame and unhappiness.

I remember one school where a staff member had received 'special' privileges over many years. Classified in a minority group and when 'sick', were permitted to take paid days off, avoiding the system's policy for sick days. That one 'special' person took unlimited paid sickies whenever they liked, they weren't sick, but life was too hard. Their leader failed to rise to the challenge and change the outcome because a precedent had been set. I found this attitude in many schools, it's just too hard, so many go for the easy path. I reported it and no one acknowledged it! Yet the principal down the road was investigated for exactly the same thing. The difference was - she was not a he.

When people cannot cope with challenges, they become anxious, leading to poor self-care and loss of focus. Usually I find they have other stuff going on in the back end of their lives. I know this because they share their personal information with me. When they cease to cope, they check out and blame anyone and everyone for their problems. I copped a lot of that! This lack of resilience and motivation builds up until it overflows, and in our department, someone had to take the fall. But for those left behind, their problems are not fixed, not in a long shot, because their behaviours remain the same. This results in those people becoming sick, depressed and take time off work. They continue not to self-care until they experience a situation out of their control and their health is affected. This happens to so many people and our statistics prove it. They invariably suffer from trauma, but they can change and improve. Post-trauma there is a life and there are methods of help and support. It's called **Post Traumatic Growth or PTG.**

Through my research I discovered an article by *Dr Meg Carbonatto B.S., M.A., Ph. D writer for the Australian Institute of Professional Counsellors, Brisbane, Australia.* In particular How to Gain Strength from Adversity 25 May 2015 www.counsellingconnection.com

Dr Carbonatto's research helps calculate PTG or **Post Traumatic Growth.** PTG is an interesting topic relevant to people in our society today and I thoroughly recommend to readers interested in behavioural psychology to research her work. She explains that there are significant growth areas of interest for people who have PTG:

1. learning new opportunities previously not available
2. finding spiritual growth
3. encountering a sense of personal strength
4. uncovering a greater appreciation for life

None of us can avoid the pot-holes on the road that we'll encounter, shit happens, it's the cycle of life. But as we run into a pothole in the road, we're reminded that all growth comes from the struggle to cope with the difficult events but not from the event itself. Our capacity to cope with adversity depends on our levels of resilience and motivation to get out of the pothole. We learn resilience and through our attitude we can build motivation which improves our strength. We must learn to problem-solve creatively to experience different opportunities. Motivation enables us to problem-solve wisely.

Those of us who are motivated to help ourselves are independent and resilient. They're the people who are self-determined, know and understand that there are many out there they can depend on and draw from their resources and networks. They ask for help when they know they need it and they're also the ones who will help others.

There is no such word as CAN'T. It's just one of those naughty four-letter words that we don't need in our lives – so get rid of it right now! Too often, we're faced with a problem that seems too big to overcome and we give up before we even try. You decide that you can't overcome a problem then you dictate your thinking to give up before you even start.

Look at successful people. Everything they seem to do is successful. Even when something doesn't work out the way they planned, they don't seem to get worried. They just move on to the next thing and become successful at that. Is this just luck? No, of course not, it's their attitude. That's what motivated and resilient people look like.

Successful people are not smarter than the rest of us; they have just learned from programming their thinking and their attitude that nothing is going to stop them from succeeding. They expect to succeed.

> *"Success breeds success."*
> **Anonymous**

A sassy attitude is the key to what sets them apart from those who would just give up or try something a little easier. Assess your own bad habits and faults. We are all guilty of waiting for the world to change for us. That is great if our attitude is positive, but what if it isn't? We will never be happy with anything we're given. Change this around and be in control of your own circumstances. Don't put change off for another day, **DO IT NOW, DO IT TODAY!**

I must admit that if it weren't for all those negative Nancies hanging around me for so many years, I wouldn't have changed my own outlook on life, and I wouldn't have grown my resilience into the fierce tool that it is today. I wouldn't have had a good hard look at myself realising that I just didn't want to be like any of them. So, it was time to change and adopt a new mantra:

> "Winners make it happen ... losers let it happen".
> **Anonymous**

My Story

My journey as an entrepreneur has been interesting. To be honest, I never thought I would end up where I am, I had great plans and dreams that I hoped would work but the reality was, I didn't have a clue what I was doing at the beginning. All I knew was that I wanted to succeed. My attitude, my enormous sense of resilience and beautiful family and friends were the only factors that got me to this point.

I once read, 'If you aim for the stars and hit the light post, be happy. At least you have hit something'. What would have happened if you had failed? The answer is easy; if you're motivated, you will keep trying and succeed at something else. Not everything you do in life will always work out for you but at least by giving things a go, you're moving in a forward direction. Believe it or not, success relies on failure and the word 'failure' is NOT a dirty word!

The only way we fail in life, is if we never learn from our past experiences. I choose not to be sad at any of my failures; I embrace them. I've been deemed a failure by others, but it's because of their negative attitudes, bullying actions and poor behaviours that I've learned to be happier with my achievements in life. I've earned the privilege to write this book, had the honour of failing and falling from my pedestal. I've been on the receiving end of brutal Facebook rants, whiners who haven't got a life, whingers with egos as big as basketballs and people who lounge around on welfare and do nothing with their lives at the expense of those who pay taxes. 'I don't have an attitude problem ... they have a perception problem'!

I've learned from each and every one of them, making me stronger and more resilient than I thought I could ever be! They opened the door to the tiger's den and released a fiercely resilient woman, I learned to unlock my voice. If we're to become highly motivated, then we need to ensure that our attitude is screwed up tight just like a bolt on the mounting under the bonnet holding down the engine to your vehicle. Motivation is about building strength to face challenges.

"Become motivated, it is within your reach."

Tracy Tully

End of Chapter Activity

What have been your failures in life? If you had your time again, how could you have avoided them?

List them below:

....
....
....
....
....
....
....
....
....
....
....
....
....
....
....
....
....
....
....
....
....
....
....
....

CHAPTER SIX

The Toolbox

"If planning is so important to our well-being and daily functioning, why is it that 25% of people pay their bills late and incur fees because they can't find their bills?"

Harris Interactive.

When you plan for a road trip, you need to be mentally and financially well organised. Advanced planning ensures your car runs smoothly, your trip takes the allocated time and you have inspiring experiences. Without planning, your road trip is full of unplanned surprises, expenses and frustrations, when it should be a time to relax, meet people, see things and go places.

You can ensure that every road trip is a great one if you plan well ahead of your departure. You can start to improve your habits by planning with as little as 30 minutes a day. Your toolbox holds all the planning resources you need to develop good habits and find the key to growing self-discipline.

Like planning a road trip, we need decisive decision making in our daily lives. To be effective in the organisation of your daily life, you need good habits. When you adopt good habits, you become organised and organised people have goals that are logical and orderly. Some good habits that organised people use are:

- They're positive and optimistic
- They're disciplined to succeed
- They're goal oriented
- They're decision makers
- They're systematic
- They **are not** perfectionists

The secret is to make small changes every day, which will slowly become nifty habits. Stick to a schedule. Left to your own devices, chances are you'll end up sitting on the floor looking through a 90's magazine that you came across on your bookshelf while looking for your road maps!

Planning to be organised is simple, but for many people, it can be daunting to action. Why do so many of us find it difficult to do something so simple? Too many of us find it hard to the point of absurd.

It's because we're not taught to systemise our lives when we were young. Remember the external control I spoke about in Chapter Three? When you were born, someone gave you attention by feeding you, making you comfortable and making you feel happy.

Everything was done for you. Then, as you grew up, you learned how to become more independent, but what you may not have learned was how to develop good organisational habits. We live in a throwaway society. Thrift shops are a quick fix to an otherwise boring outing at the shops, we can buy heaps of stuff that we might not need but we think we want. It's called clutter. We have takeaway food at our fingertips, so we don't need to cook. We have television for nightly entertainment. Without realising it, we're ditching our lives in this throwaway society.

How do we start to declutter our lives? There are heaps of apps and self-help articles available on the internet, so there's no excuse not to be organised. However, it is a matter of **deciding to do it**. A simple YES, I'll do it, is all that it takes. This means changing our habits.

It's this simple –

- **take 15 minutes daily to put everything back in its right place. Everyone has 15 minutes**
- **take 45 minutes every day after you clean your teeth to do something physical, whether it be leg lifts on your bed, stretching, squats or arm lifts with weights**
- **take 30 minutes every morning to sit with your family, eat a healthy breakfast and pack your lunch for work**
- **have kids - teach them to do the same thing while you're doing it**

It's not difficult and the benefits are immediate.
Total: 1 hour and 30 minutes.

Now, compare that with three hours watching TV every night. It's a no-brainer, right? So why aren't you doing it? The answer is simple – if you're honest with yourself, it's because you're lazy. That's harsh, but true. If we're politically correct, it's because you're procrastinating. Same thing, different words. So, what's your excuse?

Procrastinating is defined as 'postponing, delaying, dallying, deferring or adjourning'. It's self-explanatory, don't you think? When I had kids, I became a procrastinator of the highest order. I loved spending all my time watching them, playing with them, and doing activities with them – and then I went to work – which wasn't as much fun and certainly didn't bring as much pleasure. Our kids were my biggest reason for procrastination, but I wouldn't have had it any other way! I look back at the years that we brought our children into the world and tearfully waved them goodbye as they left home, ready for their own life journey. I know I could have done it differently and with all the same outcomes of pleasure and not missing a single moment of fun. I thought I was doing it well, but if I'm brutally honest – I was so stressed during that period of my life. Not because I had kids, but because I had a whole lot of other stuff happening at the same time and all competing for my attention.

Like many other mothers, I raised our two kids on my own. I didn't have a husband who came home from work every night to help. In those early years, he was away for weeks and sometimes months when he worked interstate and no mobile phones. He still is an itinerant worker. We worked hard, like everyone else, to put a roof over our heads, pay a mortgage, childcare and education, so there wasn't much left in the purse at the end of each week. Sound familiar? It's pretty much the same story I hear every day from so many other women and like most other women, I fell into the ugly trap of multi-tasking.

At that time in my life I was working in a highly volatile and time-consuming job. I was on call 24 hours a day, 7 days a week. My position was traditionally designed and developed for men, with a wife doing all the running around, shopping, washing, bringing up kids and looking after the family. I was the wife, and I didn't have anyone to run around for me. I wasn't paid well for the job, no organisational support – no such thing as bonuses or praise! Our department then and still does depend on the good nature and generosity of its employers to the detriment of family life. Working in a rural area, I was left in isolation to fend for myself with no professional strategic direction, only a supervisor who visited twice a year with a list of questions I had to answer. No sharing or caring. It was and still is **employee exploitation.**

Thirty-eight years later, the job is still the same, only supervisors visit every 10 weeks, still with the boring list of questions to answer, 30 minutes' maximum for each visit which includes a strap around the school grounds if you're lucky. My work life reflected that of my organisation – fast, constant changes that no one could keep up with and chaotic. So, be kind to yourselves, if one of the largest government organisations in the state can't get it right, how on earth should you be expected to?

Under the state's Industrial Award and Workplace Health and Safety Act, our education department does not uphold the requirements to support teachers and principals. This is serious negligence on the part of an employer who has the audacity to hold others to ransom when they can't even run their own back end. The way our teachers are treated in schools is atrocious. Teachers are granted a wee bit of time for their planning each week but that is always consumed by other tasks. If a teacher's roles and responsibilities cannot be valued by their employer then it is of no surprise that parents and students don't value them. Our state's academic results continue to annually fall behind other states. All the education department has to do is have a good look inside every single school. They can't do that because they don't have the capacity and they'd overthink it so it would take 5 years to organise.

Without that critical knowledge they can't inform their outcomes to the best of their ability and there's no progress, relying on archaic staff, student and parent feedback platforms. Teachers are in immense pain and suffering and are not afforded the time to prepare their planning and research.

A *Wall Street Journal Report* noted that office workers waste an average of 40% of their workday, because they were never taught to organise using skills to cope with the increasing workloads and demands. For every hour of planning, three to four are wasted; waiting for information, not being prepared and poorly managed tasks.

We tend to only wear 20% of our clothes, 80% of the time, the rest hangs there, taking up space. 80% of clutter in our home is a result of disorganisation, not lack of space. Make the decision, adopt good habits, schedule and systemise.

There are so many benefits for adopting good organisational habits:

1. Reduced stress
2. More time to spend with family
3. More money to save for an annual holiday
4. More clarity to stick to your goals
5. More energy to keep you alert and active

What are the costs of not doing it?

Stress is singularly the most evident cost of not being organised. By simply having a more organised system of keeping track of your bills and documents, you can help minimise financial stress-influenced conditions such as depression, anxiety high blood pressure and shingles.

When my daughter returned home from boarding school each holiday, her days were exciting - catching up with friends and being busy - as all school kids are. During her high school years, she chose to live her life by the philosophy that the greatest shelf in her room was the floor. Until one day when it all came to a halt. During the morning, I had asked her a few times to clean up her room. She had consciously failed to hear me, like all good teenagers, and the room remained in disorder. After my third pass by her bedroom door, I entered her room and took every item of clothing off the hangers and dropped them in a pile on the floor. This followed with every garment in every drawer and on every shelf. When I called my daughter, she came running, unsuspecting, to her bedroom. There she found a large mountain of clothes and shoes piled up in the middle of her room. The onset of a piercing screech 'MUUUUUUUM, why did you do that?'

Her brother and his friend came running, keen to see the action and watch what promised to be great entertainment! I calmly explained to our daughter that I had asked her three times to clean her room and she'd failed to do so. I further explained that as it was her room and her responsibility then it was also her decision not to clean it. I further explained that if she chose to continue not to listen to my directions when I asked her to clean her room, I would throw everything out of the window and turn on the sprinklers.

Then she would have to wash, iron and fold everything before she packed it all away. Her actions came with a consequence and so did my decision - just facts, no emotions! She looked at me in quiet surrender. She 'got it'. I think she was impressed with my actions and decisions! Since that day, our daughter has a highly systemised method of keeping her clothes and goods ordered and I am very proud of her. Our son stood there smiling then burst into laughter announcing that our daughter had a 'floordrobe'. That joke has been in our family ever since! Does a member in your house have a floordrobe?

End of Chapter Activity

Are you a hoarder? Do you have a 'floordrobe?'

List the things you can declutter inside and outside your home.

Minimise the mess and you will feel better, more organised and have greater focus.

....
....
....
....
....
....
....
....
....
....
....
....
....
....
....
....
....
....
....
....
....

CHAPTER SEVEN

Pot-Holes in the Road

"Any fool can make something complicated. It is hard to make something simple".

Richard Branson

In a world where everyone is struggling for more time in their lives, why is it that research is showing that procrastination statistics are on the rise?

According to some researchers, procrastination has more than quadrupled in the last 30 years. Did you know that the average attention span of adults has shrunk by 50% over the past decade?

An estimated 20 percent of people identify themselves as procrastinators. They want to start a job, business, sport, hobby or project, but they don't. Why? It could be because of a fear of failure, they don't have the money, or they're just waiting for the right moment. Usually fear of failure goes hand in hand with fear of success.

Many find fear of failure very real, with constant mind chatter making us feel anxious, nervous and doubtful. Let's face it, negative head talk is a result of too much time on your hands. If you can spend three hours surfing the internet or watching TV every night, then you have too much spare time that could be better used doing something productive. These are addictive, habit-forming behaviours that need to be broken. Bad habits go hand in hand with procrastination. Crush your laziness.

Some of the tell-tale symptoms of a procrastinator is not paying bills on time and missing activities in their life. Usually, these are the type of people who constantly leave things to the last minute to complete. I know, I'm one of those! With this behaviour comes the rush and the accompanying thrill-seeking sensation of adrenaline.

Procrastination is learned, and in my case a form of rebellion against my parents' strict upbringing. It started when I was at Uni and grew as my independence became stronger. I yearned for a life where I could indulge a carefree streak of self-expression. I found myself searching for optimism and a release from the times and yearned to experience freedom.

Friends endure procrastination because they accept our excuses, usually laughing it off as just another one of our individual traits. They grant us approval to procrastinate, by tolerating it. Family members are the same, they endure it because they have grown with it and ignore it as a personal trait that inevitably, becomes normal.

People procrastinate for many reasons. They're thrill seekers like me once, waiting until the last minute for that euphoric rush, escapers who avoid the perceived fear of failure and subsequent fear of success. These people lack effort rather than ability and usually have poor attention spans.

Some of the causes for loss of attention is attributed to certain factors: such as 18% stress, and 17% decision overload. Research has shown that an office worker checks their emails an average of 30 times per hour. Here are some statistics for the average time a person will watch a marketing video:

10 seconds or less; 89.1 %
60 seconds or less; 46.44%
5 minutes or less: 9.42%

Based on the following averages, a third of the audience is lost by the 30-second mark and by a single minute into the video, more than half the audience disappears. Finding ways to become time-effective helps us to maximize our results. www.*Treepodia.com*

Social media has the ability to addict our minds and the impact on our thinking ability is exponential; affecting our attention span and rewiring our brains. A UCLA study showed that five hours of internet surfing could change the way our brain works. Social media and internet addiction are real; students become restless, fidgety and it affects our hormones. Social networking has a chemical effect on our brains, oxytocin the hormone that stimulates trust and empathy, spikes when using social media. Stress hormones tend to drop and adrenaline is released when we respond to a sudden change in environment and social media is one of those; a series of changes, with the body sending out spurts of this addictive hormone.

Some surveys suggest that 85% – 95% of students have problems associated with procrastination. As a school principal I regularly saw this, with so much going on across so many different modalities a day, plus an ever-intrusive threat to violence, led me to feel constantly hyper-alert.

If we can learn to stop procrastinating, we will be happier with our lives. One of the biggest costs of procrastination is our health. It is one of the reasons why some university students can develop immune deficiencies such as glandular fever, flu and colds, as well as insomnia. Uni students alter their behaviour to adapt to their academic life and studies, they generally party hard and study long hours without constraints by others.

You can help yourself by removing constant distractions and adopting good time management approaches. You are your only competitor, so do it successfully. You must beat your procrastination by yourself. Research ideas, talk to others, attend workshops and seminars.

Following are some steps to solve your procrastination problems and become more productive:

1. Prepare the night before - clothes, lunch, documents
2. Exercise in the morning – 30 minutes
3. Use your meal breaks to do tasks: shopping list, pay a bill
4. Divide a big project into simple steps, with deadlines
5. Schedule your chores and stick to it

6. Work at an allocated desk at home
7. Redecorate your bedroom or a corner of the house every month
8. No mobile devices near your bed

I don't know how to start; I don't know what to do or where to go. Is this you? It was me once. Keep reading to find out how my simple system can help organise your days easily.

Two things motivate people; pain and pleasure. If you're planning on readjusting your vision, it will cause pain and it will cause pleasure. You will need a plan to manage good change and bad change. The hurdles you must jump are part of the plan. You will stumble for a while, until you get it right.

Both pain and pleasure involve emotions. Learn how to manage your emotions. Think about your current reality and ask yourself, 'Is this it? Is this as good as it gets'? Ask yourself where you want to be.

Visualise by keeping a picture of your destination in your head. Keep it bright because if it fades, then so will your future. When a bright, clear picture can be seen, turn up the volume. It can now be heard. This is the voice inside your head. Keep the picture close to you. This will bring you pleasure and start motivating your future state of mind.

There will be a lot of interruptions; you may experience fear, a sense of impossibility, financial capacity, physical transition from the current environment, grieving and constantly providing others with explanations. Initiate the resolution. What will that feel like? The answer is simple - freedom. If you have made a change in your life, it isn't 'a giving up' process. Others think it is because they get caught up in behaviour and not the intention. So, don't forget to reinforce to yourself why you're doing what you want.

You will be asked the question 'why?' a lot! The question 'why?' creates the expectation that there should be a rational explanation for everything we do. Sometimes we act in ways we can't explain, even to ourselves. If we attach our self-esteem to the action of changing our behaviour and not to the result, then we are taking back control of who we are, and we get back our energy. Most people are preoccupied in life with endings. Big government organisations make this mistake, year in and year out, with deadlines and no collective appreciation of the time needed to analyse and discuss on the front line.

Big government organisations have a structure that should have gone out with the new millennium. Large, unwieldy and top-heavy departments have organisational structures that would be better governed without the minister of the day's foot soldiers breathing down everyone's neck. Way too often, I've seen ministers who are obsessed with themselves and their delicate egos, led by petty political brown-nosing rather than doing the best job that should be done, with the correct time, people and resources. It's all upside down; our departments are full of way too many highly paid executives, with little to no idea of what it's like working in the field.

It's the journey that we must start to learn to enjoy, the time it takes to think, talk, share and develop projects or activities. There is always too much rush to meet political deadlines in these types of organisations still run on traditional methods that don't match up with modern times. The Queensland education department still beets to the industrial age drum.

In the last 10 years, it's been all about the next election. Ministers have too much influence on management of government departments and given they have no expertise in these areas, it's clearly not because of their concern for solid economic success, but rather, for purely selfish reasons - keeping voters happy and a good wage in their pocket. Voters just don't see that. The threat of calling the media 'to make a complaint' is very real, and excruciatingly painful when you work for the government. Voter behaviour directs everyone into panic mode, sending public servants with the 'glazed eye look', scampering to a defence position to minimise the perceived embarrassment on each individual politician. It is well and truly out of hand, to the point of totally ridiculous. The business of politics has become an embarrassing circus.

Help me organise my days!

I'm going to show you a *simple motivation system* to kick start your day that I use to help my daily organisation:

I have used this to:

- **Build resilience**
- **Improve motivation**
- **Break bad financial habits**
- **Lose weight**
- **Grow confidence and self-esteem**
- **Manage sickness and trauma**
- **Strengthen partnerships in business**
- **Improve networking.**

I often speak to people who've told me their number one problem in life is organising themselves daily. During these discussions, I've found they don't have just one problem, but many problems they need to solve and they feel so overwhelmed by it all.

> *"I find that my goals change as I achieve them."*
> **Tracy Tully**

Of course, I understand this feeling of hopelessness; I was like that once. Which led me to develop my own system that helped me get through each day smoothly, called my WHAT? Goals system.

It doesn't matter how old you are or where you are in your life, these goals will help you organise yourself for stress-free days. 40% of adults say that if they had more time, they would spend it with family.

1. **Acknowledge where you are today and where you want to be in the future. This will help you to visualise your dream**
2. **Start small and then progress to bigger goals as you feel more resilient and confident**
3. **When you have achieved your first big win, celebrate it! Reward yourself with something that will help you draw on in the future, if your spiral starts to descend**
4. **Recalibrate when something is going a little off course and needs tweaking**

Many years ago, I decided to give up smoking. I tried a few programmes, but they only made me feel worse. I failed twice and when those two attempts were unsuccessful, I became frustrated, I wanted to give up smoking. I developed my own **WHAT? Goals** system. I knew **'What'** I wanted to change, and I also knew that I continued to fail during my previous efforts to crush this goal. I refocussed on my previous failures in my **'How'** section and it was this action that became critical to my eventual success. I recognised the triggers I'd previously been ignoring; they were my weaknesses.

4 triggers held me back:

1. I believed that smoking helped me stress less
2. I believed smoking stopped weight
3. I smoked in the bedroom
4. I smoked my first cigarette in the morning with my coffee

I needed to get rid of 2 beliefs and 2 habits **BEFORE** I gave up smoking, *'give up drinking coffee'* I had to do this before I could even try to give up smoking. Giving up coffee became a dominant mindset and was more difficult than I ever could have imagined! I gave up drinking coffee, cold turkey. The headaches were awful but they only lasted two days. I was satisfied that I'd broken that habit and wouldn't relapse, then I listed another habit to help me beat my triggers, I removed all the ashtrays.

To my smoky brain, those were enormous challenges to face! As I mentioned earlier, too often we usually don't have just one problem to solve, we have many problems that challenge us.

The third step **'Action'** kept me on track and included a **Personalised Health Plan PHP** that I use to coach clients, you can find this on my website. My **Personalised Health Plan PHP** is critical to ensuring that I look and feel good at all times, using my simple and cheap platform, incorporating health, nutrition and fitness. It's a one-off cost with no purchase of expensive products and supplements. The

Personalised Health Plan PHP helps entrepreneurs and business owners to stay focussed and fit using their personalised epigenetic data to attain their optimal well-being. Once I had that nailed, I committed to the final step in my system *'Time'* detailing how long it would take to stop smoking. This was short and simple, two words - Stop Smoking - and I did! Of course, there was a significant reward for this!

Using my **WHAT? Goals** system to help me plan, I achieved success.

My **WHAT? Goals** plan looked like this:

WHAT Give up smoking cold turkey

HOW
- Stop drinking coffee
- Get rid of ashtrays
- Focussed mindset
- Drink water when I feel like a cigarette/hungry

ACTION
1. Name the jar for weekly savings "cigarette packet $$"
2. Eat before work and shopping
3. Personalised Health Plan – health, nutrition and exercise

TIME
- Expect cravings at 7 days, 2 weeks, 4 weeks, 6 weeks, 9 weeks, 11 weeks
- Reward – snow skiing in September school holidays

Pot-Holes in the Road

I followed my plan religiously every hour of every day. I gave up smoking cold turkey, it worked and I didn't put on weight. I have never taken up smoking since and I never will!

The up-side of this story was fantastic. I put away the money I would've spent on cigarettes each week in a jar and left it in the kitchen pantry. Our kids hated smoking with a vengeance, so they kept an eye on the growing funds in the jar. I made a reward for myself for giving up smoking and the reward I made involved the whole family. We named the jar, 'Falls Creek holiday'. The money I saved by not buying cigarettes each week added up quickly and after six months I had paid for a full week of skiing at Falls Creek for the family! If I can do it, so can you!

End of Chapter Activity

Now it's your turn!

Take a deep breath and apply my **WHAT? Goals** system to the bad habit that you dearly want to break. Don't kid yourself either, there is no good time, it's the time right now. Write down the one thing you dearly want to change. You've done the first step – the *What*. That's great! You've committed to the **WHAT? Goals** system already!

Next, write down the remaining three letters of the word **WHAT**; these are your goals to break your beliefs and habits. Under the heading *How* list all the things that you know will sabotage achieving your success. Be ruthless with yourself, don't leave even the simplest thing out. *Action* under this heading list the things that you will do; hourly, daily, weekly and monthly to keep you on track.

Now it's time to broaden your goal planning to a bigger project.

Pick a project. *Grow your Finances* is a good one adopting my **WHAT? Goals**. List the four headings but this time, make the period of time in your goal Time - as quarterly. Every three months, you will set a new sub-goal within the *Time* goal. You will then have a 12-month road map with 4 goals and underneath each goal are your sub-goals. It should be simple and brief with quarterly tasks that you can achieve.

When seeking a vision for your life, you need 4 things to happen. You need a vision, a big picture, a plan and a mentor. Everyone needs a mentor to help them on their journey. This system will guide you to work out your purpose and find simplicity, so it's got a name. The system will help lead you in the right direction, motivating you for action.

Tips and tricks to get more organised:

- **Start small**
- **Start smart**
- **Keep a chore chart**
- **Make it fun**
- **Purge**
- **Treat yourself**
- **Find a place for everything**
- **Turn it into a challenge**
- **Get rid of 'stuff'**
- **Accept that you'll never be perfectly neat**
- **Stop throwing everything in a junk drawer**

Follow the process and you will achieve success. Only YOU will stop YOU from doing it!

"Never underestimate yourself. You are stronger, smarter and more resilient than you think you are. Don't be offended if others underestimate you. If you are motivated by what others think of you, you will never be fulfilled. Back yourself and go for it!"
    Chelsea Bonner, Founder of plus size modelling agency Bella Model Management.

CHAPTER EIGHT

Running on Empty

"Our fatigue is often caused not by work, but by worry, frustration and resentment."

Dale Carnegie

Do you often find yourself saying there aren't enough hours in a day?

Are you one of those people who haven't got enough time to go to bed early, but you just need to sleep? Do you fall asleep on the couch while waiting for the spaghetti to boil on the stove for dinner?

If this is you, then you're like 80% of Australian adults. Research shows that Australia has a sleep deprivation problem. A study in by the Australian Sleep Health Foundation found that the number of sleep problems among our Aussie adults was up to 15% higher than its last survey conducted in 2010.

Dale Carnegie believes that fatigue is not often caused by work or lack of sleep, but by lethargy and exhaustion linked to numerous factors, lack of sleep being only one of them. Overtiredness contributes to our inability to sleep, due to the effects of increased use of electronic equipment and the rising dependency on social media. Lack of sleep is caused by many different medical factors as well as anxiety, constant use of electronic devices, body temperature, poor pre-sleep preparation and discipline.

Fatigue is defined as being exhausted, weary and tired and is closely linked to our self-esteem and self-confidence. If you find you're constantly fatigued, then you're not looking after yourself and you can bet your bottom dollar that you don't have high self-esteem, which affects your self-confidence.

Do you always feel like you're running on empty? No time, energy, or desire left in your day to make you laugh or do the things that you enjoy? Do you feel tired after you wake up in the morning and groan about starting a new day? Are you the person who wants to turn off the alarm, roll over and go back to sleep, every morning? Do you find yourself feeling so overwhelmed by all your daily tasks that you can't be bothered eating lunch or cooking a delicious dinner every night?

> *"Sleep is that golden chain that ties health and our bodies together."*
>
> **Thomas Dekker**

Fatigue costs us so much time in our day, because it affects our focus and that can lead to making mistakes. Lethargy or *foggy brain* is a very real issue for parents, particularly mothers with small children who are trying to do it all, including work, who must battle adjustments to their hormone levels. The feel is real.

My focus is on **fatigue** and the brain and how it affects us emotionally. Without fuel in your car, you can't travel and so, without passion in your heart, you can't live the life you want. If you aren't living the life you want, you start to feel fatigued and overwhelmed which leads to anxiety and poor self-esteem and therefore, low self-confidence.

Self-esteem isn't an attitude we learn daily at school, and for many of us, wasn't given to us by our parents or the environment in which we were brought up. There are so many people out there with poor self-esteem and with that, comes insecurities and judgement of others.

People without positive self-esteem are emotionally hurting and they not only hurt themselves, but they hurt others as well. They dump their unhappiness on others, because it makes them feel better. They want their pain to be your pain and they succeed, time and time again. They succeed especially when they see they've hurt you because that makes them feel better. These people lack empathy for others and can be demonstrating signs of mental health and possibly become sociopaths. These are the people you see trolling on the internet, haters, and can tend to be vicious stalkers. If people deliberately choose to hurt you to make themselves feel good, then they're dangerous.

Stop beating yourself up with other people's negative talk. Don't let it inside your head, trying to influence your head voice, because it will if you don't have healthy self-esteem. Who are they anyway? They're not experts! Follow your own path and don't listen to others' opinions. Their opinions should not influence your thinking, because it's not fact and they don't have any evidence, only their opinion. There's a lot of self-proclaimed *opinionators* out there! They're sad sacks and *negative Nancies.*

Negativity is powerful and can suck you right into its big black hole of insecurity, striking at the very heart of your confidence. For many, our self-esteem is vulnerable and fragile. Why do you think politicians are so quick to whinge about each other? It's a defence mechanism to protect their fragile egos! Believe me, they have egos as fragile as the rest of us.

There's nothing you can't have or achieve if you work hard and keep your focus on your **WHAT? Goals** That is your map to success. Be determined to be the person that you want to be. You are your only limit, don't let **opinionators** stop you from being who you want to be.

Keep a sharp, disciplined focus and these people will fade into the background and more than likely pursue others. Don't let unsuccessful people keep you from succeeding. Make a commitment for your life and by doing so, only you control it. Don't blame the *opinionators,* it's their problem not yours, those *sad sacks*!

Toxic people are what I refer to as *'Negative Nancies'* and I've worked with so many of them! These people never consider the consequences of what they say or their actions, because they're shallow and tend to be narcissists. Those who pose as 'know it all's', don't understand that responsibility comes with it and with responsibility comes accountability. Every action has a consequence and for every person that makes false allegations against others;

either for their own enjoyment or to entertain others, they're blind to what they do. They don't take responsibility for their nasty actions and behaviours, because they don't know how to, and they simply don't know they're toxic! They're the 'know-it-all's' who have an answer for every situation and they're never wrong! A-know-it-all is called **omniscient** and they're usually those people with some or all of the following traits: conceited, arrogant, obnoxious, egotistical, narcissistic and big-headed. They dismiss the opinions of others, their comments and suggestions because it doesn't fit their opinion.

We all make mistakes; most of us beat ourselves up about making mistakes. Perfectionists don't cope well with making mistakes, probably because they've been knocked down one too many times when they've made mistakes as a young person. Perfectionists get tired quickly and when they feel fatigued, they pass the pain onto others. Living to achieve constant success and gain admiration from others with high expectations makes people perfectionists, who can be difficult to work with.

Making mistakes is just like losing, which is all part of playing a game. Making a blunder or a slip-up is part of daily life, just like losing. The Aussie culture demonises losing. Australians are very competitive, we see this in our national sport, rugby. Losing is part of playing, but in Australia, we have a culture where losing is an opportunity to tear people down. It's called the tall poppy syndrome.

Too many parents, teachers and coaches overprotect our young people, which makes them scared to lose. This breeds insecurity, a fear of trying and lowers self-esteem and confidence.

Tall Poppy Syndrome

Bullying is deeply connected to the tall poppy syndrome, which is culturally ingrained in Australia. In modern days, it's the behaviour people use as an excuse to treat those who are deemed to be a success or have succeeded at something, to bring them down and discredit them. I experienced it regularly during my career in the last 20 years and observed it happening to others, especially women.

Wikipedia and other online sources describe tall poppy syndrome (TPS) as a term largely used in Australia, New Zealand and the United Kingdom to define a judgemental culture in which people of genuine merit are resented, condemned, attacked, or criticised because their talents or achievements appear to elevate them above or distinguish them from their colleagues. This culture is prevalent in some government organisations.

Australia's convict beginnings share a long history of the 'underdog' culture, stemming from the deep and significant effects on our nation by the English feudal system. Convicts transported to the New South Wales penal colonies suffered a deep loathing of their mother country's political and legal systems that rendered brutal and barbaric treatment against convicted prisoners, designed to physically and mentally break the convicts' will to live. This bred ignorance, jealousy and a profound hatred amongst the convict's social structure in gaols and on the ships, with a 'dog eat dog' mentality of survival. It is prolific in Australia today; it is prolific in the Queensland education department.

Researcher *James Larsen, Ph.D. in Article No. 244 Supervision Findings,* explored the destructive action of envy in the workplace. "*Australia has a problem called the tall poppy syndrome. It's rooted in their culture and it hurts their economy, but the more you learn about it, the more familiar it sounds".*

Larsen claims that success arouses envy and hostility and he believes that the Australian culture began with a shared attitude of hostility toward successful people and destructive actions and behaviours to foil them and ruin their success. Larsen believes that the economic development of Australia is intrinsically affected by 'tall poppying,' by ruining the success of Australia's most creative and energetic people which in turn, profoundly hurts the nation's economy.

This is so critical in Australia that the term **'dumbing down'** is a well-known characteristic swiftly adopted by those kids who do well academically and who are constantly ridiculed and physically abused in the schoolyard, from those who aren't academic. Given that 70% of the Australian employment population is vocationally inclined, this has been and continues to be a grave problem that's perilously ignored by government education departments which 'put their head in the sand', allowing it to continue gaining dangerous momentum and profusely flourishing in schools across the nation.

During my career in education, I endured endless hostility because of my perceived success. Our children suffered as a result of my position which labelled them 'different'. One of my daughter's primary teachers demanded she stop talking 'posh', because she pronounced the word 'dance' with a soft vowel. When our daughter explained that's how her mother spoke, her teacher replied, 'say it properly'. Thankfully, our daughter didn't **'dumb herself down'** to meet her teacher's opinions on how she should speak.

Australia was originally settled as a British penal colony, and many Australians trace their heritage to the criminals sent here. They were mostly angry and violent people, failures in British society, and the one thing they didn't like was successful people. Much of our slang is derived from convicts and its expressions and meanings are an interesting research topic. The Australian expression, the *tall poppy syndrome,* was used in 1931 by NSW Premier Jack Lang, when he described his democratic policies as 'cutting the heads off tall poppies'. Use of the term was more widely used in Commonwealth countries where British convicts settled.

In 2015, the University of Waikato in New Zealand conducted research into proving that the culture of the tall poppy syndrome might result in a decrease in the average organisational performance of up to 20%. It further defined that cyberbullying can be compared to the physical assassinations of King Tarquin's rule (died in 495 BC), the legendary 7th and final King of Rome, according to recent research by Suchitra Mouly, from the University of Auckland, Reference: Mouly, V. Suchitra and Jayaram K. Sankaran (2002) The Enactment of Envy Within Organizations. **The Journal of Applied Behavioural Science,** 38 (1), 36-56. www.businesspsych.org

The tall poppy syndrome contributes significantly to our Australian culture and it is very much alive and well in regional and rural schools in Queensland. Research by Dr Robert Funnell in 1996, Griffith University, Queensland relates institutional categorisation and order to structural and demographic factors outside school as influencing the types of curriculum and differences in educational outcomes. Likewise, his research demonstrates that behaviour management is acknowledged as a leading psychological method to reduce classroom conflict by applying 'rational choice' techniques. However, in rural schools and those with poor academic results, the methods generate unattainable strategies placing staff in difficult positions. It is the reason behind why so many make excuses and blame others.

I had the honour and great pleasure of working with Dr Robert Funnel, Griffith University on a joint paper on education policy, ***Developing and sustaining education programs that matter for remote communities. Robert Funnell and Tracy Tully January 2004.*** Together we worked on a case study at Charleville State High School, based on comprehensive demographic information in a rural and remote community. We found that the problems of sustainability of our youth in rural and isolated areas are greatly exacerbated by the nature of broad educational policy which has significant defeats in remote and rural towns. Strongly reliant on government funding to support areas in illiteracy and behaviour, we found that when funding stops, the success stops with it. **The issue with short-term funding in these areas prevents youth sustainability.** Together, we delivered strong evidence that the problem with Queensland's Education Department policy is not seen in the conditions in which they must be conceived and in which they must be set in place. Policies are assumed as 'common wisdom' and it's no surprise to me or those with an astute knowledge of rural and isolated areas that the mismatch with the economic and social conditions continues to this very day. It is now 2020 and still nothing has changed since 2004, 15 years since our paper was submitted and published.

As a principal of rural schools, I embedded highly successful pathways programmes within the local community, providing mentoring to address specific barriers to successful school-to-work transitions. These programmes and others like them, tend not to be implemented beyond regions or in rural areas with TAFE facilities. The restrictions in educational department policy were evident, when compared with focusing on the conditions, parents, students and employers face and the economic activities that sustain their existence. The **Charleville Woolshed Inc** programme and the **Outback College of Rural Education OCRE** were enormously successful, however, this is where community mentors witnessed my malicious victimisation under the umbrella of the tall poppy syndrome, cultivated by small-minded people who chopped down the poppy. Dale Carnegie's quote hit the nail on the head, my fatigue was caused by the constant resentment and plainly evident malice and spite by those less fortunate of a work ethic as strong as mine.

Through our joint research, Dr Bob Funnell and I witnessed first-hand the great successes of lifelong learning. We celebrated the knowledge that the more you grow, the more you know and the more you learn, the more you earn. Together we determined that in rural and isolated schools and their communities, great things can happen, but are thwarted by small minds, politics, minority groups and lack of knowledge. I have unwaveringly proven in my schools that there is nothing that you can't achieve, if you're willing to put in the hard work. My data proved this unequivocally. But as Gary Vaynerchuk reminds us, toxic people will bring down a good business, every single time.

Accept the challenge to be where you want to be, be grateful for what you have in life and this will give you great confidence and a wonderful feeling of achievement. Focus on your path and walk that path, by being brave. Stand tall and walk in the direction that you want to go and be FEARless. Buckle up and never stop learning to improve yourself. Feed your mind with strength and courage and you will become self-made.

End of Chapter Activity

What innovative strategies do you use to help solve your problems?

CHAPTER NINE

Fuel Up

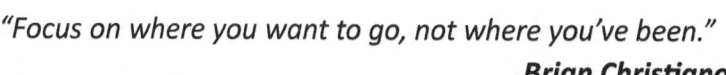

"Focus on where you want to go, not where you've been."
Brian Christiano

It's most important to focus on where you are in the present. In *Nicole Hatherly's LinkedIn article, 'Managing Life's Domino Effect' March 2017,* she refers to the powerful and hallucinating effects of the invisible need to control our lives and that of others. Of increasing global interest is the effect that social media platforms have on the addictive needs of many users who invest huge amounts of time and energy controlling the perception that others have of their lives.

Users have total control of the lives they present to the public and the outside world have grown accustomed to viewing the 'seduction' of a controlled digital life. Hatherly proposes that we're trying to achieve the unachievable if we try to control our lives and she makes reference to *The Worry Free Life* blog's interpretation of the *domino effect of life*. 'Life' being referred to as the first domino, followed by 'thoughts', 'emotions' and 'behaviours'. Events in our existence constantly change, they're unpredictable and inevitably place a hurdle in our way to navigate. We cannot control our lives, no matter how much our desire.

When we travel, we see evidence of how people have adapted their cultures, lifestyles, political and religious circumstances to their environment. History tells us that this has been happening for a millennium. So why is it that so many of us struggle to adapt to what life throws at us? Our painful thoughts and feelings exist in response to the realities of life and we draw on these to help us through difficult experiences. However, we need to separate what's going on in our five senses and what we're thinking. Our reaction to daily dramas is constantly fuelled by the media, at an incredibly rapid pace, producing within us a feeling of hypersensitivity. Thus, our creative minds constantly imagine a future that we don't want, and which may or may not ever exist, but makes us feel extremely anxious. This is one of the major reasons why anxiety levels have increased dramatically over the last decade. Not so long ago, our daily lives were slightly slower, and we weren't regularly witnessing 'of the moment', sudden disasters and catastrophes playing out across the world stage. The bombing of Twin Towers was an example of this.

As creative individuals, we generate intense inner imageries to our responses to life, which makes our behaviours take us away from who we want to be. Our well-developed creative capacity has technologically advanced to such a complex degree that we create powerful pictures of the world, about things that might or might not happen in the future, making us experience a high sense of reality that just isn't real. The relentless stream of celebrities crossing our screens, creates such a false sense of the real world to younger people who become obsessed with their lifestyle.

Increasingly, we see the reduction in people's ability to identify the trigger to their problem, because of their lack of reality. I highly endorse the emerging principles of the **Acceptance and Commitment Therapy ACT** system, which is a theory-based approach to behavioural change and attempts to explain why we get stuck in our thoughts. *ACT* focuses on the elements of behaviour change and guides us to concentrate on being present to help us to adapt to what life throws at us. This is a system that is well worth researching on the internet.

For some, it's very easy to look at our lives and feel like the past has a strong hold on us. In our minds and hearts, this can happen to the point of preventing us from moving forward in our lives. Our mind and heart are two different entities; the mind can change in accordance with exactly what we want, and the heart is governed by our emotions and reactions to events around us. Changing our mindset is a process but changing our emotions is so much harder. The reality is, if you wish to change, then you need to have the power to act, to make the change.

Our history has a fundamental impact on us, whether it's good or bad, it's our past. Our mindset is the strongest tool we have to make any change we desire, and we can programme it to let go of the past, minimising the impact on our future.

The Power to Act

"It's tough trying to move forward, but the hardest part is deciding not to stay."

Tracy Tully

Anyone can dream about starting a new journey and moving forward in their life. But are you doing it? Are you planning your new journey? If your answer is *'No, I'm still dreaming about it'*, then you need to finish reading this book! If you're honest with yourself, it's probably because you're too scared to make a move and you have a lot of excuses why you can't move forward. Moving forward requires action. Action requires a new mindset.

I've found that the most difficult decision of all is having the power to act, especially if you're not sure how. Having the power to act means that you need to leave your comfort zone. Your comfort zone is safe and predictable. You don't have to do anything that pushes you to take a risk. Taking risks frightens many people and the perception is that risks are scary. Living in your comfort zone is a mindset, you're not going anywhere, and your dreams aren't going to happen, unless you change it. Stepping outside your comfort zone and making a definite decision to leave is critical to starting a new journey. So, no excuses, no 'ifs or buts', because your 'butt' is behind you and we're moving forward. Your time has come, get off your butt!

Connect to your Passion

Discover your way forward and produce a better tomorrow for yourself, because you can do it. Keep reading and I'll show you how you can equip yourself with the power to act, to change your circumstances and change your mindset.

Passion about the things that excite you connects to your drive, so engage the gears and move forward, because too often we ignore our passion. Why? For many different reasons; fear, lack of confidence and self-esteem, feelings of guilt, feeling selfish, no time and lack of money. Sound familiar? The list goes on and on, because we always find an excuse!

When you allow your passion to overrule all these feelings of sabotage, you will find the power of your inner strength to follow your purpose. Be fearless and FEAR less! It's ok to feel passionate and follow your purpose. Allow your excitement to lead you. The exhilaration will give you the strength to feel the connection.

Forget what others think about your desires to play with your passion. Negative people always have a reason to distract you from pursuing your dream. Why? Because they can't have the same fun you're having. Be true to yourself. What do they know anyway? It's your passion and no one else can judge. If others are always making excuses for you and judging you, stop listening to them, it's only their opinion, not fact.

End of Chapter Activity

List five of your favourite passions.

How would you use them to provide a better life for yourself?

CHAPTER TEN

Snap Shots

"People call me a perfectionist, but I'm not. I'm a rightist. I do something until its right, and then I move on to the next thing."
James Cameron

Are you a **perfectionist**? Do you struggle with frustration and feel overwhelmed trying to make everything perfect? Do you feel anxious when things don't go the way you planned? Then you probably have felt the fear of imperfection, which is where you find yourself avoiding situations where you might make mistakes, setting impossible standards for yourself. You'd rather do nothing than do something incorrectly. And it can take over your life.

"Atelophobia is defined as the fear of not doing something right or the fear of not being good enough". *April 2019, Atelophobia/Huffpost* www.huffpost.com

What's happening around us socially and economically?

As a country, we've had little success in improving relationships, yet we are concerned enough that we spend a lot of money trying to improve it. In Queensland, in public education alone, millions of dollars are spent on improving school success against the national average, without significant improvement, no matter how success is measured and no matter how hard we are persuaded that it's happening. It is in this type of environment that we need to take a good hard look at our structures and foundations across our nation and states and adopt a new psychology and new structures.

"Fear is educated into us, and can, if we wish, be educated out"
Karl Augustus Menninger

In December 2013, Queensland schools were given a fail mark by the Newman government advising that, *"Education chiefs have made the extraordinary admission that Queensland's school system is failing kids and flagged a massive overhaul. In a damning document, the Education Department admits 'Queensland's education performance is not good enough'"*. Tanya Chilcott Courier Mail 22 December 2013.

"Queensland Schools slipping behind other states on literacy and numeracy tests." Courier Mail March 14, 2013 Tanya Chilcott, Rob Kidd and Kate McKenna.

In 2015 we read, *"Queensland students most improved NAPLAN test takers but remain behind the national average."* ABC News 5 August 2015 Matt Wordsworth

Snap Shots

In the *2018 online Qld Government site 'The Challenge for Queensland'*, we're advised that, *"The retention and performance of students in STEM education is critically important for the futures of young people and the success of Australia's economy. The evidence shows there had been a dramatic decrease in the number of students undertaking science in secondary school... Along with the reduction in numbers of students in these subjects there is further finding that Queensland is 'substantially behind the performance of our East Asian neighbours at all education levels'. This is most keenly exhibited in primary aged students and Indigenous students".*

"Queensland not only scores poorly compared with the rest of the world, but also with the rest of Australia in the key STEM subjects of science and maths. As few as 49.9% of Queensland students achieved at or above the proficient standard in scientific literacy at a Year 6 level." The Queensland Government Office of the Queensland Chief Scientist last updated 12 June 2018.

We don't fail to notice what this significant and steady decline means in real terms, both socially and economically. We know we're not the 'Smart State', our embarrassing Queensland tag for over a decade, to foil the world with false bravado and blatant deception.

In October 2018, we read, *"Queensland's rise to top education performer could provide a model for the country." ABC News 23 October 2018 Julie Sonnemann and Peter Goss.* Oh dear! The title was decidedly deceptive to the reader, giving a false impression that Qld education could be the national role model and who reads past the title anyway? It's not until the third paragraph, *"Qld makes one month more progress on average in numeracy and two months in reading once background is taken into account",* we find the statements are made in regards to primary reading and numeracy and that Qld is in fact still behind the states nationally.

It is this constant veiling of the truth, massaging and protecting delicate political egos that allows critical facts to be distorted. It is this culture across Australian states by politicians, government sectors and the media, that aggressively promotes and idealises the tall poppy syndrome, projecting it into our homes daily, the use of print and radio media brainwashing our youth by irresponsibly validating and promoting bullying.

It stands to reason that if our country is socially and economically running in chaos, then it's not so surprising that the general population is feeling the same way. It's certainly not surprising that public school students in Queensland are failing because of diminished belief in themselves. The Queensland education department is charged with the enormous responsibility of educating thousands of young minds per year, but readily conceals the truth and openly deceives the public, and will continue to fail, as has been demonstrated for the last four decades. This avoidance of finding a real solution for their failure permeates throughout our culture and with the aid of the media, saturating the way we think.

Why is it that everyone would have us believe that our school students are failing? They're not, they're only as good as the system that educates them. The big F word – failure, goes to our government leaders, NOT OUR STUDENTS. They're the ones who are failing our students. They're failing our students because they will not be honest and acknowledge the in-depth problems and recognise that everything they have done historically does not work and they need to find a real solution immediately.

The ART of opportunity

Over the last nine years, I've learned some of the most valuable lessons of my life. What seemed to be impossible situations, led to the rise of unforeseen and exciting opportunities. They presented as mountains but those opportunities took some time to 'see', cloaked in fog masked by government corruption, fraud and just plain gutter filth.

Finding opportunities in impossible situations took **time, tenacity and termination**. No, it's not a spelling error and it isn't determination, its **TERMINATION**. Termination is as powerful as the pause!

The 3 T's took **time** to research, truckloads of **tenacity** to 'show and tell' and required **termination** of all that I valued and believed. But out of the ashes sprouted the shoots of opportunity and this is how it's done.

The **ART of opportunity** is a system designed with the following three elements we need, to help strengthen ourselves and make the most of impossible situations.

1. Time to adapt and adjust
2. Tenacity to react and respond
3. Termination of values and beliefs

The **ART of opportunity** is designed to use powerful, commanding and influential words to our psyche. The power of these words helps us reject fear, motivating us to **ACT** and become resilient. Their ability to help us rise above the challenge, trauma or bullying you've experienced is powerful. I remember a time when I used the word *'minutiae'* meaning *'details, finer points, particulars'* in a senior leadership meeting. I was asked by perplexed staff members what the word meant. I explained its meaning and the context in which I used it. What struck me the most was not that no one knew the meaning of the word, but that not one single person looked it up on their mobiles, to satisfy their knowledge and contribute to their learning, but rather, they chose a 'put down' saying that I used words that were too difficult for them to understand! The blame game again.

Time to adapt and adjust

We must learn to adapt to change and **adjust** how we recalibrate our GPS of behaviours and actions. Not to 'dumb down' and turn the lights off but to **'brighten up'** and turn the lights on. When taking a journey on a road less travelled, we fit out our vehicles with some major necessities, such as spotlights, bull bars, extra water, a second spare tyre, jumper leads and spare fuel. We do this so we can quickly adapt to difficult situations if they arise that may prevent us from completing our journey on time! Travelling on a difficult road in dusk, it makes sense to turn on and adjust your spotlights so you can see clearly and avoid trouble ahead. In life, if we **'bright up'** and turn the spotlights on, then we're able to see clearly and adapt to an impossible situation this gives us the ability to swiftly adjust our GPS to avoid 'potholes in the road' and provide us with the most accurate direction of where we need to go.

Tenacity to react and respond

We must learn to be **reactive** to difficult situations and find within us the ability to respond quickly and with purpose. I often hear people tell me they freeze in certain situations and feel fearful, finding it impossible to communicate or act. Especially when speaking publicly, entering a room full of people, walking into a party alone etc. Being able to respond adequately can not only save your life when you're on the road travelling in difficult terrain, but also in difficult situations. Being **reactive** with the ability to respond will help you search for opportunities in all difficult situations. Teaching yourself how to react in difficult times and respond promptly trains our brain to cope. We must be **tenacious** in our ability to protect ourselves and those we cherish.

Termination of values and beliefs

The world is not always a good place, and there are sinister people and situations out there. If you lack **tenacity** and the ability to **terminate** toxic people from your life, you may be chewed up and spat out by those who are expert at hurting others. **Terminating** those beliefs and values that deceive us by taking advantage of our compassion, roles and responsibilities that hurt us.

Some people are wired with a mindset that lives, breathes and anticipates drama. These people have programmed their thinking into believing that drama is normal. If they wake up and there's no drama, they make it happen by turning a situation into one of chaos and drama! It's a dangerous cycle that leads to negativity.

We have a system that, like all systems, is flawed. It's flawed because it relies on human decision-making, which can err on the side of bias, favouritism and unfairness. The world is not a fair place and life is not simple. When individual opinions and decisions are made, there is always room for prejudice and discrimination. We see it every day in our newspapers and on our streets. The **#MeToo** campaign is growing traction as more and more people are finding their voice and speaking out against sexism, discrimination and assault. I'm adding to that, the **#digitaldamage** campaign.

End of Chapter Activity

The Bum Barger

We have owned a few businesses over the years, some good and others not so good. We developed all our own businesses, but one in debt and neglected. Upon my arrival, I noticed a few older staff weren't happy with some of our decisions that took their power away over the other staff. One was signalled to me as a bully and I watched with great interest at the way they treated others, especially those they perceived as weaker than them.

In a couple of our businesses, we employed backpackers. The bully didn't like them, was always angry when they arrived for work and was constantly finding fault with them. They openly detested them working for us, regularly running them down and making up dramas about them. They were toxic and swiftly caused problems within the group.

One day one of our backpackers came to me and said that he'd been bum barged at the kitchen sink. I asked him to explain and he told me that every time he washed the dishes, they came over to the sink and threw their hips into him, half knocking him over. He was very serious and as I discussed it with him, he further explained that they spoke nastily to him and made him feel hopeless. I described back the action of the 'bum barging' to ensure I understood. I said to him, "I knew it! I thought they 'bum barged'! They did it to me too. I thought they just had a big bottom, so dismissed it the first time. After the second time, I realised that it was probably deliberate". I described how they 'bum barged' me and he said, "Yes that's it! That's exactly what happened to me!"

I waited by the sink washing the dishes, keeping the perp in my peripheral vision. I didn't really believe they'd do it again and honestly thought it was just an action of a big bottom in a small space, wrong time, wrong place. Sure enough, they came in for another 'bum barge'. This time I was confident they were on a mission to deliberately 'bum barge' me. Time to apply the ACT system; adjust, respond and terminate. I waited as they lined up to launch at me, a fierce look on their face, an armload of greasy pots and pans and a bum ready to knock me over. As they approached, I kept washing and chattering away nonchalantly to the others in the kitchen and just as they were ready to collide with me, I was handed a knife and took a swift step back to put the knife safely on the bench. They came flying at me and with no goal post to hit, kept flying past the sink until landing on the ground face first, covered in greasy food scraps, oil, pots and pans!

That poor young fellow couldn't believe it! He was so frazzled with anxiety caused by this tormenter; being in a foreign country and believing that it was our culture to bully people by 'bum barging'. He told me that he froze every time the perp approached and fired their missile at him. He wasn't able to eat or sleep, it was a very difficult situation for him, but he needed the work and didn't want to leave.

As time passed, other staff approached me with similar nasty stories and so it was farewell to the toxic 'bum barger'! After their departure, everyone breathed a sigh of relief! He was so relieved, and I was able to teach him not to accept bullying behaviour and how to manage bullies in the future. I was regularly regaled with stories by the other staff over the following weeks of the 'bum barger's other antics, so it was a good outcome from a bad situation.

Snap Shots

List a situation you have found yourself in where someone bullied you

CHAPTER ELEVEN
Traffic Infringement

"It is not the critic who counts; not the person who points out how the strong man stumbles, or where the doer of deeds could have done them better. The credit belongs to the man who is actually in the arena, whose face is marred by dust and sweat and blood; who strives valiantly; who errs, who comes short again and again, because there is no effort without error and shortcoming; but who does actually strive to do the deeds; who knows great enthusiasms, the great devotions; who spends himself in a worthy cause; who at the best knows in the end the triumph of high achievement, and who at the worst, if he fails, at least fails while daring greatly, so that his place shall never be with those cold and timid souls who neither know victory nor defeat."

Theodore Roosevelt, US President, 23 April 1910

I wrote this book for me and it has taken a lot of time and thought to finish. I nearly didn't. It's my responsibility to share my story, facts and evidence that I know to be correct. There is not one other person who is an expert on my story; I am the only person with all the evidence and data, no one else. Someone encouraged me to write the real story, the hard and painful truth about a few things that happened to me as a high school principal employed by the Queensland education department. Its purpose is to inform my family, friends and those colleagues treated disgracefully because of their friendship with me, to remind us that life does get better.

My book is a **legacy for my children and their children**. I owe it to them and it's my responsibility to our family's future generations. It is singularly the hardest thing that I've ever done in my life. It's the only way that I know to ensure that our kids have the real story and no one can take that away from them, ever. Too many malicious people, employed or linked to the Queensland education department, took their childhood lives away from them.

I'm a critical dialogue disruptor by having a voice in the **#MeToo** arena because it's the right thing to do and I'm not afraid to speak out. I challenge small thinking and talk out loud about issues people want to keep hidden. As a positive activity following a horrendous experience and at the urging of my family; I wrote this book aimed at the **#digitaldamage** and destruction to my family and particularly our children. To those people, excuses will always be there for you, but opportunity won't.

The **#digitaldamage** caused by each corrupt and deceitful officer of the Queensland department of education plus those they chose to incite with their malicious actions, must be heard and considered as a **RECOMMENDATION FOR CHANGE** of the **Queensland**

Traffic Infringement

Public Service Act and the conduct of Queensland government departments under its administration. Serious criminal conduct has been directed against myself and many others, by those whose actions and behaviours defy the legislation and the Westminster principles which govern this Nation. Department of education officers and non-government people solicited false and vexatious allegations against me without cogent evidence, this is referred to as libel. My family and I endured a witch hunt of enormous proportion.

Education department employees across the state experience regular verbal abuse, threats of violence; violence against themselves and family members, by students, parents, and guardians and anyone else who feels like jumping on board the 'complain train'. As principals, we witness and manage online paedophile groomers and trollers, violent assault, tragic death and bereavements, rape, suicide, murder, incest, drugs, bullying, fetishes and community paedophiles. Research released in May 2020 from the Australian Catholic University and Deakin University found 1 in 3 Australian Principals have experienced physical violence and threats from parents and students. I've also witnessed it from principals, teachers and regional office employees, P & C Association members, council employees and cultural groups. Victimisation, discrimination and Australian bullying – our nation's culture.

State school principals are exploited, unpaid shift workers who slog away well over the standard hour week in accordance with the PSA and Industrial Award. We have little if any supportive leadership and work during school holidays and Christmas. This is employee exploitation yet the department, union nor any principal association can ensure real change that prevents this blatant exploitation which is at a critically serious level. A state industrial relations issue and mockery of natural justice. Police, health, fire and emergency services workers are paid overtime; we are not. School 'holidays' are used for school work. We do not have trained support systems or trained leaders for our violent and drug-fuelled circumstances. The preposterous and outrageous Public Service Act is deliberately and maliciously abused without care or intervention and the newly elected party in the 2020 elections with guidance from the Qld Crime and Corruption Commission CCC need to act immediately to put an end to it all. This won't happen under a Labor party led government.

Our department culture revolves around 'who likes who'; a typical primary school mentality, nepotistic and bullying. Ethical Standards Unit officers' conduct is disgraceful, scandalous and unchecked - clearly obsessive, irrational, unskilled emotionally and unable to manage difficult conversations with the communication demanded for their jobs. They were gifted the right and responsibility of my career, my family name and my life. They have not only failed me, but every other officer who comes under their management. Egotistical ex-police officers who bully others for their own self-satisfaction.

Their roles and responsibility were to ensure confidentiality and safety to me, their employee, they failed in every aspect. Intentional denial of essential information and deliberate refusal to authorise me adequate time to access my emails and documents to prove my innocence. Physical standover tactics in regional offices, isolation in my home, distressing pursuit by trolls and media, treated like a criminal, witch hunted by complainants and their friends, failure to protect me and my family, empowering the spiteful treatment of our children, all with the calculated intent to cause fear, humility, confusion and to push me to resign from my position. This was and still is, corruption at its best, uncivilised harassment and abuse and it's happening right now. It's no surprise that my Egyptian friends are horrified to hear this story is happening in Australia, it's far from normal and the cover up is over.

Tom Barlow in the role of Acting Director-General, authorised approval of a Courier Mail article published on 12 January 2012, knowingly flouting the PSA and Privacy Act by misleading Courier Mail journalist, Tanya Chilcott, that I had been suspended from duties due to physical abuse and other false allegations that were printed, despite his knowledge that there was NO documented evidence of these allegations ever. This article tagged me for life and was an utter load of bullshit pumped up to feed his inflated ego with the intent to sow the seeds to the public. When mud is thrown, it sticks. Barlow intentionally committed libel "a published false statement that is damaging to a person's reputation; a written defamation" (Oxford Dictionary); knowingly and maliciously authorising corrupt false evidence to another party. This is libel and is permanent **digital damage** against my name and that of my entire family. **The damage to our children's lives is utterly inexcusable and must be endured for the term of their natural lives.** NO government officer has the right to play god, ever. This was reported to the CCC.

I'm constantly appalled by the criminal conduct, negligence, incompetence and politically biased actions used against me and our children. I was ignored by the Premier's Office when my mother, sister and I divulged the physical abuse with evidence of a witness, contravening the Privacy Act and criminal conduct at the hands of my supervisor - it was shrugged off. When asked, 'by what law did the supervisor have the authority to go through my personal belongings?', yet another shrug. The officer represents Premier Annastacia Palaszczuk, who failed to act on written evidence of criminal actions and behaviours by an executive officer against myself with witness statements and whose leadership is on a swift descent into corrupt economic decline.

The **#digitaldamage** to myself and my family's name will follow us into generations to come. I am unable to expunge this **#digitaldamage**. I was unable to defend myself, my family and our name during my employment. I am not in that position anymore; your time has come.

IT'S TIME FOR CHANGE

Traffic Infringement

End of Chapter Activity

What changes do you think your work organisation would benefit from?

....
....
....
....
....
....
....
....
....
....
....

What strategic innovative activities could you develop to engage these changes?

....
....
....
....
....
....
....
....
....
....
....

CHAPTER TWELVE
Destination Known

"Your body is priceless, treat it with care. It's your vehicle to travel through life."

Tracy Tully

It's important to remember that there's nothing in life you can't do. You can achieve whatever you want, if you're willing to work hard for it. It's also important to remember that nothing is free in this life, and those who have succeeded, have invariably worked hard for their great success. You are your only limit, no one else. It's not anyone else's fault where you find yourself today. You must take control of your life and accept the challenge to be where you want to be.

Stop making excuses and blaming others, it becomes the heavy baggage you drag around on your back. Let go of it, accept where you are right now in your life and make the decision that you want to take responsibility for where you want to be. Be grateful for what you have, every single day.

The Power of a Pause

> *"Between stimulus and response there is a space. In that space is our power to choose our response. In our response lies our growth and our freedom."*
>
> **Viktor Frankl, Auschwitz survivor**

Stephen Covey's book, *7 Habits of Highly Effective People* (1990) referred to Frankl's quote almost 30 years ago. Dr William Glasser, *Choice Therapy Theory – A New Psychology of Personal Freedom* (1998) together with Covey have been profoundly dominant in my life, influencing my beliefs and teachings over the last 40 years as an educator. Both authors empower their readers with tremendous insight and understanding, describing the complex behaviour of humans.

'There is power in a pause – a lot of power', Cedar Barstow states. *The Power of Pausing: Why You Should Give Yourself a Break* February 21, 2019 GoodTherapy.org blog article. Barstow explains that 'a pause is simple, invisible and a marker between stimulus and response'. He is no stranger to Covey and Frankl. His words convey understanding of the integrity of being both present and mindful.

Do we know what it means to be mindful? We are repeatedly told to be mindful every day, but what does it mean? Does it mean that we need to meditate every morning, perhaps adopting the 'downward dog' pose and finding our chakras while ohmming into the early morning hours?

> "The power of the pause intends us to be mindful, which influences our happiness."
>
> **Tracy Tully**

I believe that through the power of choice and choosing the life we want; we can choose whether we'll be happy or not. We all have the choice to do what we want.

The word 'intend' means to have purpose. The word 'mindful' means being conscious and focusing our awareness on the present. It's logical that by being intentionally mindful, we consciously focus on our awareness of the moment. If we take time out to pause in our busy day, we grant ourselves power over our ability to be mindful, giving us a strong feeling of gratitude, contributing to our sense of well-being and happiness.

Do you know how to do that? No? I didn't either until I was raced to hospital in an ambulance with very high blood pressure. It wasn't until I reached my tenth year of mentoring that I discovered that it isn't just about listening, profiling a client or providing strategies, advice and guidance. I learned that it's all about enabling a client to talk about their issues and struggles, whilst paying explicit attention to the moment when they **pause in their story**. That was the significant breakthrough for me and a special moment in my journey in mentoring.

The power of the pause is intriguing because it clearly demonstrates a time when the speaker is consciously considering the purpose of their story, rather than offloading and telling the story to make themselves feel better. Do you have the willpower, resolve or grit to observe **the power of the pause** in your thinking? Have you ever tried it? How do you discover **the power of the pause**? Do you learn it by stopping mid-sentence, while you're drinking your coffee, as you gallop around the kitchen strapped to your scalding mug of aromatic eye opener and checking your mobile for messages?

The act of pausing is a very profound and influential strategy which I use to help those coming back from trauma or bullying. The intention to be mindful demonstrates to you that **the power of the pause** in your life is truly remarkable in helping you turn your life around after difficult times or challenging situations.

Some things stopping you from pausing in life:

- **Addictions** – they don't have to be a hard-line habit. Addictions can seem small and irrelevant to the benefit of our daily lives. Do you want to save money? Many of us aren't very good at it! Being unable to save money, like smoking, or the mother's evening ritual 'little helper', eagerly poured out of the wine bottle and scoffed down with the gusto of a thirsty child, is an addiction and one that we can change. The power is in our minds. It's our behaviours and actions that determine whether we will save that 50 dollar note each week towards our annual holiday, smoke that lunch time cigarette, scoff down that bottle of wine every night, suck our tenth espresso coffee for the day, or snap the top off 6 beers each night. They are addictions and many of us have one or two or have had one at some time during our lives. Many of us will deny we have an addiction – it's usually the drinkers and the smokers! Nah!!!

They're not addicted, they can give up any day, whenever they want! But they can't and they don't.

- **Relationships** – who has a perfect marriage or relationship? Relationships are hard work and it's easy to overlook others' needs in the fast pace of our lives.

- **Exercise** – who finds it easy to jump out of bed and do 20 squats, lift weights for 30 repetitions and stretch those quads?

- **Nutrition** – who eats a perfectly balanced breakfast every morning, every day, while racing to get to work on time?

- **Sleep** – Who consciously goes to bed early every night to ensure they get the adequate hours of sleep that leads to a healthy life?

My favourite tips and tricks for learning how to pause in life

Learning to pause - you must start at the smallest level possible, learning how to develop the habit of pausing. The trick is to make your very first pause at the start of the new day, when you wake up in the morning. Rather than jump out of bed to greet the new day, **pause until you are fully awake**. You will know when you're fully awake because your eyes will focus on something in the room. When you're fully awake, you feel a sense of lucidity that a new day has started. This may or may not be a good thing. Lie in bed breathing slowly by deeply inhaling in through your nose and exhaling your 'sleep air' out through your mouth. It's that easy. Well, if it was, we'd all be doing it wouldn't we? We don't though, do we? This is the very first micro-step that you must achieve at the beginning of every day. This is what I call a *pause,* which when accomplished every morning, becomes a *habit.* Making a conscious effort every morning to pause and deliberately controlling your reactions to wake up, gives you immediate power over your body's response when you wake.

Know your learning style – when we learn something for the first time, whether it's a skill, fact, algorithm or habit, we learn best by using our own unique style. Learning styles influence us more than we realise because they direct us in the way we learn. Learning styles change the way we internally characterise experiences and even the words that we choose.

There are 7 different learning styles:

1. **Visual (spatial)** you prefer using pictures, images and spatial understanding
2. **Aural (auditory/musical)** you prefer using sound and music
3. **Verbal (linguistic)** you prefer to express yourself using both the spoken and written word
4. **Physical (kinaesthetic)** you prefer using your body, hands and sense of touch
5. **Logical (mathematical)** you prefer using logic, reasoning and systems
6. **Social (interpersonal)** you prefer to learn in groups or with other people
7. **Solitary (intrapersonal)** you prefer to work alone and use self-study

Destination Known

Each learning style uses different parts of our brain to process knowledge or skills. Key areas of our brain are responsible for each learning style. By involving more than one style when we're learning, we remember more of what we learn.

What learning style are you? Find your learning style through the *free learning styles inventory* by using the online questionnaire at https://www.learning-styles-online.com

Like everyone else in history, setbacks have been a part of my life and I'm comfortable with the feeling of turbulence. I understand that commotion and disorder go hand in hand, whether we want it or not. You're not the only person on this earth who will fail; everyone's a failure at some point or other in their lives, the only true failure is when you decide to give up.

Create and follow your own path, be curious and explore new situations and places. Travel and seek new sensations. Reward yourself with the opportunity to explore and learn more. Challenge yourself to grow. Don't try and change others; you will get distracted and lose your focus.

My goal in life, is to be 'in pursuit of happiness' or according to our kids, my 'karmic self-maintenance'! The years have rolled past with the good, the bad and the bloody ugly. I survived those tumultuous times by rummaging around my brain every morning for a few remaining cells, then strapped them to a bunch of bitter coffee beans and bucked them out around the kitchen, whipping them into action until I was super charged. Many years ago, I gave up smoking and as I explained earlier, the coffee had to go! Mornings now are more sedate, with a teabag waved over hot water and a spoon of sugar; one of my last vices along with chocolate and vodka!

My destination is clear; to enjoy my friends, meet new ones, age gracefully and continue to keep learning, travel, eat chocolate and drink vodka whenever I want! I believe it's expected of me that I go on some sort of long mandatory trek down the track, as I choose to leave the road less travelled.

> *"Confidence is walking into a room full of people and not having to compare yourself to anyone."*
> **Tracy Tully**

Be thankful for all the struggles you've gone through in your life, because they do make you stronger, wiser and more modest. Don't let those difficult situations break you, let them make you.

> *"We travel because distance and difference are the secret tonic of creativity. When we get home, home is still the same. But something inside our minds has changed, and that changes everything".*
> **Jonah Lehrer TheAnthrotorian.com**

Those who walk through the fire leaving sparkles of inspiration in their wake, are the only ones who can stand outside the fire in the cold with the wolves, glowing with confidence and courage. Be one of those.

Make a declaration to yourself that it's a beautiful thing to be able to stand tall, put a smile on your face and sashay along the path admitting to yourself, 'I fell apart and I survived'! When you start taking care of yourself, you will start to feel better. When you feel better, you will act with confidence and you will attract like-minded people and when that happens, you've earned the keys to open the lock on the door to your new journey. It all starts with you.

THE END

To the Queensland State Government and people of this nation;

it's time to critically review the Queensland Public Service Act PSA and all government departmental Ethical Standards Unit practices that harmfully thwart basic human rights and natural justice, preventing employee well-being, especially during Emergency Situations; resulting in corrupt, deceitful, negligent behaviours and actions.

Under the Queensland Public Service Act PSA, all employees stood down on investigation, deserve the basic human right to:

- ➢ Receive a signed Statutory Declaration by every single person who commits to making formal allegations against others

- ➢ Regular and qualified consultation, communication and support ensuring protection of the mental health and well-being of all employees

- ➢ Access to ALL files including computer data and correlating technology in an adequate and timely manner, to effectively support their evidence

About The Author

Tracy Tully is a disruptor and change influencer. A Personalised Training Coach, mentor, award winning international speaker, author and two times whistle-blower for the last 30 years. She's a motivation percolator, wordsmith and distiller of fear; an expert in building resilience, providing you with the power to unlock your voice and make better decisions in your life, turning overwhelm into passion.

She creates influential speakers all over the world, by helping people unlock their voice, lifting their Profile, Presence and Profit. She teaches confident conversations by overcoming fear through motivation and resilience, funding a lifestyle working anywhere in the world.

A purveyor of inspiration, Jill-of-all-trades in mastering fear, building courage and strengthening resilience; her key message is:

> *"Life is like a box of chocolates, each sweet delicacy can be likened to a goal, enticing you to keep moving forward. But in every box, there will always be one or two chocolates you don't like. I will show you how to find the sweet spot in everything you think of and do! Most of the battle is achieving the right mindset."*

FEARless Buckle Up … Build RESILIENCE, is Tracy's first non-fiction book, sharing her true-life experiences, exposing corruption, deceit and exploitation as a two-times whistle-blower; inspiring her heroic prose, **"She Rises from the Fire"**.

Her first children's book, **Gordon the Goat and the Gully Kids** has been a lifelong passion and her third book, **Queens in Sandcastles** is due for release in 2021.

Tracy's held senior leadership roles in the public, private and non-profit sectors for the last four decades and is renowned for her strategic and innovative problem-solving. She will candidly show you the reasons why there is no room for assumptions, blame or procrastination in your life.

Tracy challenges people to step out of their comfort zone, building their resilience muscle! She believes understanding an assertive mindset engages focus and commitment, firmly believing that the only competition you have is yourself.

About The Author

"Your PB or Personal Best, holds the key to improving individual performance through developing motivation, strengthening resilience, gaining confidence and planning more effectively and efficiently."

Tracy Tully

Hailing from a strong and fiercely loyal Defence Force family and born in Penang Malaya, Tracy lives in Queensland and has spent a lifetime observing people across remote, isolated and rural areas, from the east coast to the west coast and across the Top End to the bottom end.

Her vocation spans almost 40 years, stretching from wild frontier towns in the Pilbara country in Western Australia, across to Nhulunbuy in the Northern Territory, onto the Gulf of Carpentaria and down to south-west Queensland. She delights in entertaining her audiences with witty excerpts, sharing her views on life. A practical, no-nonsense woman, Tracy calls it like it is, *'a spade is a spade and not a bloody shovel!'*

Tracy's relatives were pioneer families in NSW; settlers searching with hope in unfamiliar and volatile frontier lands. They faced many challenges driving their families, provisions, horses and stock, deep into a vast, unknown and unexplored continent, facing soul-destroying experiences, tragedies, unpredictable extremes in weather and a harshness of insurmountable odds that sucked the life from their souls.

Mother of two and married to Bob, member of the vast Tully clan, original Irish settlers Patsy Tully and Sarah Durack, pioneers in the 1870s who travelled north of Melbourne in bullock drays loaded with all their worldly possessions. They embarked on a better life in the vast, unpredictable channel country, in south-west Queensland.

We live in the lucky country protected by our native Indigenous people who traversed this land in ancient times, to the courageous pioneers before us.

Always open to an opportunity that knocks on her door, Tracy is fearless in her belief in herself. She makes no apologies for her candid nature by indulging in a carefree streak of self-expression. She believes that, *"living is all about enjoying every moment of your life, no matter how rocky the road gets. Life is way too short, so don't waste your time worrying about what others think".*

She teaches that there will always be pot-holes in the road to challenge you, no different to what was experienced by the early settlers and believes that many people are unable to cope in modern times, due to their lack of resilience.

Tracy is a strong advocate for leaving the highway and taking the road less travelled, because the reward far outweighs the risk.

You can book a 1:1 **Finding Your Sweet Spot** session with her at www.tracytully.com

MEDIA:

- MAMAMIA
- Landline
- ABC Longreach
- Courier Mail
- The Country Life
- Toowoomba Chronicle
- Western Times
- Warrego Watchman

Acknowledgements

I would like to thank those who supported and guided me to finish this book, following through on the whole process of planning, writing, edit, layout, printing and cover preparation. What a wonderful journey it's been!

I honour famous author Christobel Mattingley, my beloved library teacher at St Peter's College in Adelaide; who inspired me with her glorious voice and infectious passion for story-telling, igniting the fire that led me to find my vocation as an author. Mrs Mattingley was a much-admired author of 55 books during her lifetime, including biographies, Aboriginal history and children's stories; a tireless supporter of education, social and environmental causes; awarded the Order of Australia and two honorary doctorates.

Thank you to the Ultimate 48 Hour Authors team: the fabulous Natasa Denman and husband Stuart, Vivienne, Lendy, Nikoli, Velin and Hayley! I look forward to publishing my next book!

Thank you to my fellow authors Joy, Dr. Jo, Niomi, Alysia, Nia, Sarita and Jane for making this book come to life!

In a world with a population of over 7.7 billion people, I laugh heartily whenever anyone tells me that the world is saturated with self-published books! There's plenty of room for millions of more books! There's something very special about a paper book, the thrill of the title on the spine, the intrigue of the cover, the smell of printed paper in your hands, the ease it slides into your bag to be read on a long distance flight and the flush of excitement of a relaxing late-night journey tucked up in bed travelling to another place or time, until sleep claims the day. Ancient Egyptians forged the path in world history through their creation of papyrus scrolls, hieroglyphics, symbols and cartouches used to preserve and portray an ancient life spanning three thousand years.

The honour of writing a book and leaving a lifetime message for others in the future, is paramount in my journey through life.

Motivation and Resilience for Women MRW

This book is about helping build resilience through motivation to face your challenges. People of all ages can feel overwhelmed by the simplest of tasks. Many don't have the confidence and courage to face every day difficult situations.

Tracy Tully, founder of **Motivation and Resilience for Women MRW** and **Confident Conversations**, has a deep understanding of the need to grow our resilience. **MRW** started on the dining room table in 2011 and continued to grow as a result of Tracy's experience in counselling, knowledge and understanding of resilience.

In her 38-year career as educator, Royal Life Saving Society Instructor and Lifetime Member of ALL Ladies League and Women Economic Forum, Tracy encountered many women who searched for the baton of resilience to protect themselves and help them navigate in a male dominated society. Observing women of all ages and cultures, she recognised that strong resilience was the one tool that guarded a woman's world from exploitation, abuse and manipulation. Her years of duty as an educator revolved around many coaching and mentoring sessions with those women who endured unfathomable behaviours and actions against them and for those who sought guidance to succeed against all odds.

That is not the story of this book, that will come later and is sure to become a motion picture. This book has been written from the learnings of those controlling and enduring experiences that developed in Tracy, the powerful credibility of her profound resilience.

Tracy delivers online courses in **Speaking Confidently** and new Entrepreneur Programmes offering exclusive **Membership Lounge** and networking group opportunities.

www.tracytully.com

Tracy provides an option b website for those who wish to share her free tips and tricks in building resilience, motivation, communication, isolation and confidence.

Readers may contribute without the hustle of sales.

www.mrwcoaching.com

- **facebook.com/mrwcoaching/**
- **instagram.com/motivationresilienceforwomen/**
- **pinterest.com.au/motivatingresil/**
- **linkedin.com/in/tracy-tully-3879a2122/**

Speaking & Workshop Opportunities

Tracy is available for speaking opportunities and conducts powerful and witty speeches, identifying and making best use of learning to instil confidence, improve motivation, strengthen resilience and assertiveness to move forward. Her presentations are passionate, motivated and highly engaging!

As a critical dialogue disruptor and change influencer, she challenges people to work outside their comfort zones, looking outside the square and retraining old and outdated thinking. Everything she does is to build your resilience, giving you the power to influence your own life. For great success to occur, it's necessary to review our attitudes through an impartial lens. That is what she does.

TOPICS:

- *Finding your sweet spot!*
- *Calibrate your mindset and find true north*
- *WHAT? Goals - you need them!*
- *UNLOCK your voice ... Get out from behind the door!*
- *From chaos to confident conversations*
- *That C word - commitment*
- *Who said the road is smooth? Build RESILIENCE*
- *Release the brakes ... STOP resisting change!*
- *Take the road less travelled - seek your passion*
- *Be a fearless warrior - battle your mindset*

Contact Tracy Tully to discuss speaking opportunities for your business or organisation on:

- +61 0429 992 916
- info@tracytully.com
- www.tracytully.com

For bookings and bulk book sale enquiries

Bulk Buying and Customisation

Are you considering a reward for business presentations, staff or clients to inspire their passion?

Tracy Tully author and public speaker offers her book

FEARless
Buckle Up ... Build RESILIENCE

as a unique opportunity to develop resilience and motivation in others

It can be packaged and beautifully presented with your product colours

Please contact us via info@tracytully.com for more information about customisation opportunities and bulk package prices

www.tracytully.com

Interested? For more information, bookings and bulk book sale enquiries:

- info@tracytully.com
- www.tracytully.com
- www.mrwcoaching.com

Bonus Offer

Mindset Roadmap 5 Steps to Success

Discover the 5 steps to success, by changing your mindset and setting it on the path you want to travel. How to deal with overwhelm, anxiety, making decisions and creating influence.

Access my useful resources to becoming a Confident Speaker

Download the link below:

www.tracytully.com

Online Programs

If you enjoyed *FEARless Buckle Up ... Build RESILIENCE* and you're searching for further information to help empower you, you're probably wishing you'd like to learn more?

Tracy guides you to unlock your voice by building your resilience through motivation and confidence and you can benefit through the delivery of one of her online programs!

www.tracytully.com

Search the MENU under COURSES

Online Programs

UNLOCK YOUR VOICE PACKAGES
Guide to being an Influential Speaker by Lifting your Profile, Presence and Profit

CONFIDENT SPEAKING PROGRAM
28 Day online program
2 Webinars
Membership to our exclusive Facebook Group
For our Speaking Circle Clients
Opportunity to speak at an EVENT

INFLUENTIAL SPEAKING PROGRAM
2 Hour Mindset Consult
4 Month online Program
2 Webinars
Exclusive Members Lounge ticket
1 Day workshop and speaker opportunity at a STATE EVENT
Brisbane, Melbourne, Sydney or Perth
Free ticket to all National or International Workshops

MASTER SPEAKING PROGRAM
As above PLUS
2 Day Workshop in Brisbane, Melbourne, Sydney or Perth
OPPORTUNITY TO SPEAK AT AN INTERNATIONAL EVENT

DISCLAIMER

The information in this book is designed to provide helpful information on the subjects discussed. This information is not meant to be used, nor should it be used, to diagnose or treat any medical condition. For diagnosis or treatment for any medical condition, consult your own physician. The publisher and author are not responsible for any specific health or mental health needs that may require medical supervision and are not liable for any damages or negative consequences from any treatment, action, application or preparation, to any person reading or following the information in this book. References are provided for informational purposes only and do not constitute endorsement of any website, books or other sources. Readers should be aware that the information in this book may change, post-publication.

The information in this book when not stated as opinion, is reported as fact and all evidence has been provided and reported to the Queensland Crime and Corruption Commission CCC.

Class Action

If you have been subject to corrupt actions and political libel under the Queensland Public Service Act or Queensland Department of Education and wish to pursue a Class Action, please submit your information to the following:

Mr Chris Neville
Condon and Charles Lawyers
P.O. Box 45
Toowoomba, Qld 4350
Email: reception@condoncharles.com.au
Phone: 07 4617 8100

Bibliography

http://bullyout.com.au/category/bullying.statistics/

Whatisbullying/Factsandfigures (August 11, 2017)

www.SafeWorkAustralia (August 7, 2018)

Cambridge English Dictionary

Max Weber Kolleg, *'a zero-sum game'* Centre for Advanced cultural and social studies. Universitat Erfurt (13 November 2019)

Mouly, V. Suchitra and Jayaram K. Sankaran, The Enactment of Envy Within Organizations. *The Journal of Applied Behavioural Science,* 38 (1), 36-56. www.businesspsych.org (2002)

www.gingergorman.com.

https://en.wikipedia.org

Changing Patterns of Mortality in Australia, 1968-2017 Australian Bureau of Statistics 3303.0.55.003 (30/11/2018)

www.beyondblue (2019)

NobleOak Life Limited: PureProfile Survey(December 2017)

En.Wikipedia.org/wiki/Fear

https://epdf.tips/would-you-like-attitude-with-that-no-limits-no-excuses-no-ifs-no-buts-just-attitude

Dr Meg Carbonatto B.S., M.A., Ph. D writer for the Australian Institute of Professional Counsellors, Brisbane, Australia. How to Gain Strength from Adversity (25 May 2015) www.counsellingconnection.com

www.learning-styles-online.com

www.Treepodia.com

Robert Funnell and Tracy Tully, Developing and sustaining education programs that matter for remote communities (January 2004)

Australian Sleep Health Foundation (2017)

James Larsen, Ph.D, Article No. 244 Supervision Findings

Atelophobia/Huffpost www.huffpost.com (*April 2019*)

www.learning-styles-online.com

Nicole Hatherly, LinkedIn article, 'Managing Life's Domino Effect' (March 2017)

Stephen Covey, 7 Habits of Highly Effective People (1990)

Dr William Glasser, Choice Therapy Theory – A New Psychology of Personal Freedom (1998)

Notes